Just the Two of us

Entertaining Each Other

Just the Two of us

Entertaining Each Other

Isabel Hood

foulsham

The Publishing House, Bennetts Close, Cippenham, Slough, Berkshire, SL1 5AP, England

Foulsham books can be found in all good bookshops and direct from www.foulsham.com

ISBN-13: 978-0-572-03220-3
ISBN-10: 0-572-03220-X

Cover photograph © Andrew Sydenham

A CIP record for this book is available from the British Library

The moral right of the author has been asserted

Printed in Great Britain by St Edmundsbury Press, Bury St Edmunds, Suffolk

Contents

*To the Saturday Night Porker, my companion in life,
in the kitchen, and at the table*

Acknowledgements

An enthusiastic guinea pig is undoubtedly a cook's best friend and my deepest appreciation must undoubtedly go to Philip Hood, my Saturday Night Porker, whose phenomenal appetite, discerning palate and boundless creativity have contributed so greatly to this book. But there are others whose involvement in my life has had far-reaching results and I would therefore like to thank Chris and Ann Lane not only for their generous friendship and robust encouragement, but most particularly for their splendid lateral thinking, which spun me around to face in a totally unexpected direction; Tracey and Mark Sanderson for their loyalty, proactivity and impeccable professionalism, which turned many a catering nightmare into a roaring success; my aunt, Sheila Bate, for making so many things possible, and Wendy Hobson, for her willingness to take a risk.

our repas de deux

A *pas de deux* is defined as a sequence for two dancers, a step for two. This book is about creating a *repas de deux*, a repast for two diners, a meal for two.

The average family, it would seem, consists of two adults and 2.5 children, which is perhaps why the average recipe almost invariably 'serves 4' or 'serves 6'. And how frustrating it can be for those of us who are outsiders, who do not belong, who do not fit the average, but are merely a household of two adults – or perhaps a single person looking for ideas for an intimate *dîner à deux* – always to have to adapt the average recipe to our needs! I have so often halved the quantities in a recipe for four and then found that the final dish just didn't have enough flavour or body – and yet when I have tried cooking the whole recipe, it has been delicious and well balanced.

How do you divide 'one egg'? Does the 'good slug of brandy' required to deglaze the pan in which you have just cooked two steaks instead of six need adjusting? What does a third of 'a bunch of parsley' amount to? Too much and your supper tastes like grass; too little and the aromatic herbiness and interest vanishes into thin air. Half, let alone one third, of the ingredients for a sauce may not purée properly in the food processor – it is more likely to end up all over the bowl with the blades whizzing around crazily on their own. Are you tempted to halve the cooking time as well as the quantities? Do so at your peril! That half shoulder of lamb will not be cooked to perfection in half the time, and it may be dry long before the other components of the dish, which expected to be cooked with a whole shoulder, are ready and have developed flavour. Half a soup recipe for four is somehow never quite enough for two, while a halved risotto recipe seems to need more than half the specified quantity of stock.

And the only way to find out is to give it a try, to have a go and learn from any mistakes. But mistakes – while useful as a way of learning how not to do something – are just a bit exasperating when you are tired, hungry, fed up, bankrupted by the purchase of expensive ingredients, or simply in need of relaxation and a good meal to put life to rights again. And when you have an important someone arriving in half an hour for that very special candlelit *tête à tête*, a mistake can become a catastrophe.

Admittedly, a bit of common sense is sometimes all that is needed. And experience is invaluable: my years of cooking professionally have certainly taught me to spot possible pitfalls in recipes, and given me a strong intuitive sense of what might or might not work if a specific recipe or ingredient is divided or multiplied. But this is of scant help to the home cook who merely wants to enjoy good food and the process of preparing it.

There is, of course, an easy and straightforward alternative, which is simply to cook the whole recipe and then eat the leftovers on another occasion – and we do that often. But what a real joy it is to come across a recipe for two that requires no re-calculating, no dividing, no improvising, no guessing; that can be followed to the letter and relied on to produce a *repas de deux*, destined to feed no more, and no fewer, than two hungry people.

Having married late in life and chosen not to have a family, the Saturday Night Porker and I have been executing a *pas de deux*, stepping out together in life, and cooking mostly for each other for some twenty years now – I say mostly because I am not counting the meals I prepared during my time as a professional cook and caterer.

Fifteen years of my life were spent providing glamorous food at parties large and small, from private dinners, directors' lunches and Ascot picnics to weddings, product launches, themed events and corporate rooftop barbecues. As 'Chef to the Connoisseur', I cooked – often with the SNP's help and from our own small domestic kitchen – for up to 400 people. That was a different world of food, which I no longer inhabit, and a different world of recipes: it was food calculated not so much to nourish, comfort, excite and stimulate, but to impress, to envy, to attract attention and to make a statement. And alongside that world existed a second, parallel one, a *pas de deux* world populated only by our cosy twosome.

Our love of food and eating, avid curiosity and infinite enthusiasm for the cuisines of the world resulted in constant exploration and testing, and in trying out new books, recipes and dishes virtually on a daily basis (and particularly on Saturday nights, when at least eight or nine different dishes were prepared and consumed – hence the salutation Saturday Night Porker!). In our *pas de deux*, we have therefore cooked recipe after recipe for four or six or however many; we have divided the quantities by two or three or more; and this has often worked perfectly well. But it has also NOT worked in the least bit well countless times, and we have been left wondering why there are so rarely any recipes for two people, why food writers always seem to aim their writing at families and dinner parties, and where, oh where, are the *repas de deux*?.

So, over the years, I have created my own collection of *repas de deux*. The sources of these recipes are as diverse as the dishes themselves: memories of my Latin American childhood; ideas brought back from our travels; creations born from reading hundreds of cookbooks and restaurant reviews or sparked by dishes eaten in restaurants; experiments with ingredients in my own kitchen; general culinary research; even a wander around the local farmers' markets. All of these influences automatically planted seeds in my imagination – to be mulled over and played around with, looked at in this way and that, tried and retried and accepted or rejected, and finally developed into a recipe for two, a *repas de deux*, ready to be tested on the SNP.

At this stage, I must add a word of warning. The SNP and I have good, hearty appetites. We love cooking; we love eating. We do not see food as something to be picked at and pushed around the plate: we consider it a friend, not an enemy. We believe that it must nourish, satisfy, sustain and

interest, and we have no time whatsoever for nouvelle cuisine-sized portions. I must therefore specify right from the start that all the recipes in this book feed two hungry, healthy, even greedy people! And this is perhaps a good opportunity to mention the fact that we have an inordinate and insatiable passion for garlic ...

There are two further, very important factors that influence my cooking. Firstly, food's health-supporting and health-enhancing properties play a hugely significant role in my kitchen. Food scares and particularly fashions abound, and what is scientifically proven, tried and tested one year is contradicted and turned on its head twelve months later. One expert assures us that a vegan diet will bring us longevity and boundless vitality; another leaves no doubt in our minds that we must eat meat and dairy products to avoid sagging muscles and thinning bones.

Over the years, I have tried many different ways of eating: I have been a vegetarian and a vegan; I have been a member of both the high-protein and the low-protein brigades; I have eaten 75 per cent of my food raw, and I have given macrobiotics due attention; I have banished animal fats from my life, and drunk two pints of full-cream milk a day; I have combined my food correctly and incorrectly. And my conclusion from all my experiments is simple and straightforward: the most energising diet for life as far as I am concerned is very high indeed in raw food such as salads, fruit and sprouts, and made up of REAL, WHOLE, FRESH and NATURAL foods, free from chemicals, pesticides, preservatives, modification, manipulation, irradiation and any other rubbish people have thought up in order to 'improve' flavour or nutritive value – and thereby further commercial interests!

Proper food requires no improvement – nature gives it to us perfect, whole and complete. All we need do is treat it with love and care. So buy fresh, whole, organic food, take it home with you, make it into a delicious meal, and eat it with joy and gratitude. Above all, have fun. And because treats are good for us every now and then and definitely part of the joy of cooking, I have included a handful of puddings for special occasions and, even more importantly, for when your soul is crying out for an indulgence!

Secondly, 'food miles' are becoming an increasingly serious issue. I admit that we eat oranges and bananas all year round, that I love mangoes and pineapples, that tomatoes feature in my salads and cooking whatever the season, and that my life would not be the same without avocados. However, when I was doing some research for an article on apples recently, I was staggered to find that a major local supermarket stocked eleven different kinds of apple, of which just one was English – and this in spite of the fact that our English orchards were groaning under the weight of some of the best apples in the world. Food that is transported across the world will have been picked while unripe and have little to offer in the way of flavour, texture or true nourishment, however seductive it looks. What's the point of eating strawberries from Chile or asparagus from Thailand in December? They may be firm and brightly hued, but they will have travelled in a barren, chilled environment for days if not weeks and never have been offered even the hint of an opportunity to achieve their full potential.

But try buying English asparagus in May, or strawberries in July, from a farmers' market or perhaps a box scheme, and your taste buds will be rewarded with incomparably fresh, seasonal produce that will probably have been picked no earlier than that very morning and will have travelled just a few miles. It will be bursting with flavour, fragrance, juice, antioxidants, vitamins, minerals and therapeutic properties. You will also be enabling small, local, specialised producers to make a decent living instead of supporting voracious conglomerates with shareholders to satisfy and fat-cat bonuses to finance. The organic farmer who supplies me with fruit and vegetables faxes me a weekly list of what he will be picking and harvesting on Friday, and my menus for the coming week will be based on the contents of the box he leaves by my kitchen door. The same goes for dairy products and meat, which I buy at local farmers' markets or from co-operatives. Furthermore, I have found shopping in this way cheaper than going to a supermarket, and is certainly far more fun and even educational.

And so to my *repas de deux*. I have divided the recipes into three categories to fit into *pas de deux* in the twenty-first century. My life during the week entails juggling countless tasks and demands on my time, and by the evening my only culinary concern is usually to get a sustaining and nutritious meal on the table before I run totally out of steam. However, while speed may be the top priority in this case, I believe in enjoying everything I do, no matter how pressed for time I am, and a quiet half hour in the kitchen putting some supper together is a delight.

So in the first section, the *pas de deux* steps out into what might be called the Quickstep, as we prepare quick, easy and delicious food at a fast and efficient pace. The key feature in the Quickstep is minimal preparation – the chopping, slicing, grating and basic preparation part taking a maximum of 30 minutes, although the actual cooking may take longer (which gives you the chance to have a shower before supper). The Spaghetti with Pickled Lemons, Olives, Oven-roasted Tomatoes and Parmesan Cheese is a perfect example, as there is very little preparation involved but the tomatoes have to roast for 45 minutes.

Some days, I seem to finish whatever I am doing that bit earlier and find I have a whole hour or so to spare and I can play around in the kitchen for that bit longer. I can even perhaps indulge in some prior preparation, such as grilling (broiling) (bell) peppers, and then come back to finish off the rest later. Evenings like this bring some balance and a vague memory of leisure. So the *pas de deux* slows down into what I call the Foxtrot.

And then there are the times – usually at the weekend – when the *pas de deux* slows down into a graceful Waltz. This is when I can relax and enjoy, spending however long it takes – an hour or two, even the whole day if I want – pottering around the kitchen and truly melting into the luxury and the process of creating wonderful food.

So join me in my *pas de deux* in its three different forms, from the quickly prepared dishes in the first chapter, gradually slowing down as we progress through the book, until we reach the longer cooking and/or more time-consuming *repas de deux* at the end.

notes on the recipes

- Do not mix metric, imperial and American measures. Follow one set only.

- American terms are given in brackets.

- All spoon measurements are level unless otherwise stated: 1 tsp = 15 ml; 1 tbsp = 15 ml.

- Eggs are large unless otherwise stated. If you use a different size, adjust the amount of liquid added to obtain the right consistency.

- Always wash, peel, core and seed, if necessary, fresh foods before use. Ensure that all produce is as fresh as possible and in good condition.

- Seasoning and the use of strongly flavoured ingredients, such as onions and garlic, are very much a matter of personal taste. Taste the food as you cook and adjust seasoning to suit your own taste.

- Can and packet sizes are approximate and will depend on the particular brand.

- All ovens vary, so cooking times have to be approximate. Adjust cooking times and temperatures according to manufacturer's instructions.

- Use your own discretion in substituting ingredients and personalising the recipes. Make notes of particular successes as you go along.

- Always use fresh herbs unless dried are specifically called for. If it is necessary to substitute dried herbs for fresh, use half the quantity stated. Chopped frozen varieties are much better than dried. There is no substitute for fresh parsley and coriander (cilantro).

- Use whichever kitchen gadgets you like to speed up preparation and cooking times: mixers for whisking, food processors for grating, slicing, mixing or kneading, blenders for liquidising.

- Always preheat the oven and cook on the centre shelf unless otherwise specified.

the quickstep

The Quickstep is described as a modern 'joy' dance. The basic figures are simple, the rhythm bright and snappy, the tempo and character carefree, vital and energetic. The pace, however, while not a full gallop, is certainly a canter. These *repas de deux* are perfect for hectic days when, for example:

- you encounter several sets of roadworks
- there is ice on the track
- you have been running just to keep up and yet still fallen behind
- you have to queue at the supermarket checkout until your feet hurt
- you decide to answer the telephone even though you've already put on your coat and are about to walk out of your office
- you forget to do the shopping
- the video machine isn't working and you want to watch a programme that starts inconveniently early
- your partner was supposed to be cooking but is nowhere to be seen
- the avocados are about to go off and you can't bear to let them go to waste
- you realise you are only human and just want to cook something quick and easy

The emphasis in my Quickstep recipes is economy of preparation. I do not give a specific time for my recipes, because no two cooks cook in the same way or at the same rate. But all in all, this is fairly fast food, involving a scant amount of messing around and fuss, let alone energy, even though in some cases, as mentioned earlier, there may be a longer cooking time involved. Some recipes are just a sauce and I have suggested various quick and easy uses for them. Lemons Pickled in Salt and Lemon Juice is the only recipe that cannot be turned into a meal of some sort but, as you will see, it often pops up elsewhere in the book.

Nowadays 'pesto' seems to apply to virtually any cold, oil-based, herby sauce. The original pesto from Genoa (made using a pestle and mortar, hence the name) is based on basil, garlic, olive oil, pine nuts and Parmesan cheese, but many other herbs, nuts, cheeses and oils make excellent pestos. However, delicate herbs, such as chervil, make an insipid pesto, while strong herbs like oregano, marjoram and rosemary are too aggressive.

Mint is very easy to grow – so easy that it's best to plant it in a container as it has a tendency to take over every inch of ground! The pumpkin seeds give the sauce a lovely texture and crunch. You can use Mascarpone or cream cheese if you prefer, but the goats' cheese brings a welcome piquancy.

This pesto is excellent with any lamb dish – roast lamb, grilled (broiled) lamb chops, a cold lamb sandwich, lamb kebabs. It's also lovely mixed into warm new potatoes or carrots, and as a simple sauce for grilled fish and chicken.

mint pesto with goats' cheese and pumpkin seeds

30 g/1¼ oz mint

1 garlic clove, peeled

20 g/¾ oz fresh goats' cheese

75 ml/5 tbsp olive oil

15 ml/1 tbsp white wine

Sea salt and freshly ground black pepper

30 g/1¼ oz pumpkin seeds

Place all the ingredients except the pumpkin seeds in the bowl of a food processor and process until fairly smooth.

Add the pumpkin seeds and process again until the seeds are just broken down but not totally pulverised – keep some texture to it. Check the seasoning.

 This pesto is best served fairly soon after it is made as it tends to lose its colour and vibrant flavour if stored for more than a couple of hours. But, since it is so quick to make, this is hardly a problem.

See also Black Grape, Pink Grapefruit and Goats' Cheese Salad (page 22).

Try this pesto with any kind of stir-fry: king prawns (shrimp), slivers of pork or chicken, and vegetables such as baby sweetcorn, strips of (bell) pepper, sliced leeks and spring onions. Swish it in off the heat, just before serving, or use it as a delicious dressing for an orange, melon and cucumber salad or for a couscous and dried fruit salad.

coriander, cashew and coconut pesto

30 g/1¼ oz creamed coconut, chopped or coarsely grated

15 g/½ oz fresh coriander (cilantro)

1 garlic clove, peeled

1 small green chilli, halved and seeded

1 spring onion (scallion), coarsely chopped

100 ml/3½ fl oz/scant ½ cup toasted sesame oil

Juice of 1 lime

100 g/4 oz/1 cup roasted, salted cashew nuts

Sea salt and freshly ground black pepper

The creamed coconut needs to be soft in order to give the pesto its lovely creamy consistency, so start off by heating it very gently indeed either in a small pan or in a glass or china bowl over a pan of simmering water.

When it is soft and malleable, place it with all the other ingredients except the cashews and seasoning in the bowl of a food processor and process until smooth.

Add the cashews and whiz it up for a few more seconds, just to break down the cashews without losing their texture. Season to taste.

 The pesto will retain its flavour for a day or two but it will start to lose its vivid green colour within a few hours.

See also Egg Noodles with Coriander, Cashew and Coconut Pesto (page 51) and Roasted Root Vegetables with Coriander, Cashew and Coconut Pesto (page 169).

Tapenade, like pesto, comes in many guises. It started out as a chunky Provençal sauce made of black olives, capers, garlic and anchovies, traditionally served with boiled vegetables. Today, a tapenade merely needs to be pungent! You can fold it into some olive oil mashed potatoes or use it as an omelette filling; or mix it with some fresh breadcrumbs as a topping for baked fish or tomatoes. It also makes a wonderful sauce for cheese ravioli or on a baked sweet potato.

green olive and oregano tapenade

75 g/3 oz green olives, stoned (pitted)

1 garlic clove, peeled

3 anchovy fillets

30 ml/2 tbsp fresh oregano leaves

15 g/½ oz fresh flatleaf parsley

A pinch of cayenne pepper

Juice of ½ lemon

75 ml/5 tbsp olive oil

Sea salt and freshly ground black pepper

Place all the ingredients in the bowl of a food processor and process until fairly smooth.

 The tapenade will keep well for a week in a glass jar in the fridge.

See also Parma Ham, Parmesan and Tapenade Crostini (page 26), Chicken with Olive Tapenade, Boursin and Pancetta (page 96) and Caramelised Onion, Tomato and Olive Frittata (page 74).

Pickled lemons are a mainstay of Moroccan cuisine. They are sold loose in large vats in the souks and added to salads, vegetable dishes and tagines – even nibbled on their own as an aid to digestion. Their flavour is distinctive, sharp and piquant, providing a welcome contrast and foil to spices, strong herbs, richness and oiliness.

Although jars of pickled lemons are available in most large supermarkets, they take just minutes to prepare so it is well worth making your own. Conventionally, they need to mature for at least a month, but the following recipe, adapted from Paula Wolfert's *World of Food*, produces pickled lemons in 7 days and the pickling liquid can be used again and again.

lemons pickled in salt and lemon juice

2 unblemished organic lemons

75 g/3 oz sea salt flakes (not crystals)

Freshly squeezed juice of 2 lemons

Wash and dry the lemons, cut them in half and then cut each half into quarters.

Layer them up with the salt in a 250 ml/8 fl oz/1 cup glass jar, then pour in the lemon juice.

Cover tightly with a plastic or plastic-coated lid and leave to mature for at least a week at room temperature, giving them a good shake every day.

To use, rinse the lemon pieces well, and scrape off and discard the pulp.

 I always keep a jar of pickled lemons in the fridge – a bit of chopped zest will give sparkle and bite to any number of dishes.

See Spaghetti with Pickled Lemons, Olives, Tomatoes and Parmesan (page 56), Roast Fillet of Lamb with Warm Minted Couscous Salad (page 48), Avgolemono Soup with Pickled Lemon Relish (page 65), Chicken with Apricot, Raisin and Pickled Lemon Chutney (page 148), and Grilled Salmon with Tunisian Vegetable Confiture (page 140).

No holiday in Greece is complete without eating the traditional Greek salad at least twice a day! It makes its dutiful appearance at midday and in the evening, either as a first course, as part of a mezze or, together with chips (fries), as a crunchy, tangy and herby accompaniment to virtually all meat and fish dishes.

But Greek salata offers so many other possibilities. Chop all its lovely Mediterranean ingredients into small dice, add plenty of fruity olive oil and you have a dressing, sauce or salsa, whatever you wish to call it. Good old Greek salad suddenly has countless uses: with hard-boiled (hard-cooked) eggs; as a pasta sauce; as a salsa to go with lamb chops or a grilled (broiled) chicken breast; spooned into baked potatoes; stirred into warm red kidney beans or chick peas (garbanzos); mixed into rice; or quite simply served on toast.

greek salata
with fresh herbs

125 g/4$\frac{1}{2}$ oz plum cherry tomatoes, quartered

50 g/2 oz cucumber, seeded and diced

1 garlic clove, peeled and crushed

20 g/$\frac{3}{4}$ oz red onion, peeled and finely chopped

10 black olives, stoned (pitted) and halved

15 ml/1 tbsp chopped fresh parsley

15 ml/1 tbsp chopped fresh mint

2.5 ml/$\frac{1}{2}$ tsp dried oregano

45 ml/3 tbsp olive oil

Sea salt and freshly ground black pepper

50 g/2 oz Feta cheese

Place all the ingredients except the cheese in a bowl, adding seasoning to taste, and mix gently.

Crumble the cheese over the top and the salata is ready to use.

This recipe does not keep particularly well as the tomatoes and cucumber tend to go a bit soggy, but you can certainly do all your chopping well ahead of time and assemble the salata at the last moment.

See also Seared King Prawns with Greek Salata (page 24), Cretan Lentil Purée with Greek Salata (page 53), Grilled Swordfish with Greek Salata and Skordalia (page 90), and Sweetcorn Blinis with Smoked Salmon and Greek Salata (page 77).

Figs, indigenous to Syria, were revered by the early Hebrews as a symbol of peace and plenty, and are one of the four historic Mediterranean foods, along with olives, grapes and wheat.

I never bother to peel figs, but there is a rather charming Italian proverb that admonishes you to feed the skin of a fig to your enemy and the skin of a peach to your friend – so it's up to you! This is a breakfast made in heaven – simple, sensuous, perfect – but feel free to have it for pudding if the fancy takes you.

figs and raspberries with honey and yoghurt

Greek honey

450 ml/³/₄ pint/2 cups Greek-style plain yoghurt

4 ripe purple figs, quartered

200 g/7 oz raspberries

Add honey to taste to the yoghurt (but keep it on the tart side to bring out the sweetness of the figs).

Gently mix the figs with the raspberries, drizzle them with a little more honey and eat with the yoghurt.

This fresh, highly aromatic salad makes a lovely first course to get the taste buds going. You could also serve it as a lunch dish with some bread but, by our standards, it would be a very light lunch indeed! The savoury bite of the goats' cheese really brings out the sweetness of the fruit and the peppery bite of the rocket.

black grape, pink grapefruit and goats' cheese salad

1 large ruby grapefruit

50 g/2 oz rocket leaves

15 ml/1 tbsp olive oil

Sea salt and freshly ground black pepper

200 g/7 oz black grapes, halved and seeded

75 g/3 oz fresh goats' cheese

1 quantity of Mint Pesto with Goats' Cheese and Pumpkin Seeds (see page 16)

Peel and segment the grapefruit over a bowl to reserve the juice.

Divide the rocket between two plates.

Using a fork, whisk the oil and some seasoning into the reserved grapefruit juice. Drizzle over the rocket.

Arrange the grapefruit segments and grapes on top of the rocket, crumble the cheese over, and top it all off with a large spoonful of pesto.

 Serve any remaining pesto on the side.

Peas and mint are natural partners. Add some French beans, crumbled pancetta and shavings of cheese and you have a bright, punchy salad, full of fresh flavours, which takes minutes to prepare: you can be shaving the pecorino while the beans and bacon are cooking and you will have the salad on the table in no time.

french bean and pea salad with pancetta

6 pancetta rashers (slices)

125 g/4½ oz French (green) beans, topped, tailed and halved

125 g/4½ oz frozen peas

25 g/1 oz red onion, peeled and finely chopped

30 ml/2 tbsp olive oil

10 g/scant ½ oz fresh mint leaves, coarsely chopped

Sea salt and freshly ground black pepper

40 g/1¾ oz Pecorino Romano cheese shavings

Heat the grill (broiler) to high and grill (broil) the pancetta about 10 cm/4 in from the heat until crisp.

Transfer to a plate lined with kitchen paper (paper towels) and leave to cool slightly.

Cook the beans in plenty of salted boiling water for 4 minutes. Add the peas and bring back to the boil. Drain and refresh under cold running water.

In a large bowl, mix together the beans, peas, onion, oil, mint and seasoning to taste.

Crumble the pancetta over the top, sprinkle with cheese shavings and serve immediately.

 If you serve this salad with some bread, it is almost a meal in itself.

Bags of raw, peeled, king prawns can be found in the frozen section of most supermarkets and, although expensive, they are priceless when it comes to fast food – so long as you remember to take them out of the freezer in good time. They are incredibly versatile and can be turned into a delicious meal in minutes.

In this recipe, the heat of the frying pan will bring out the wonderful aromatic herbiness of the salad and melt the cheese just enough to make it all unctuous and savoury.

seared king prawns with greek salata

45 ml/3 tbsp olive oil

200 g/7 oz raw king prawns (shrimp), shelled and deveined

1 quantity of Greek Salata with Fresh Herbs (see page 20)

Sea salt and freshly ground black pepper

Heat the oil in a large frying pan, add the prawns and cook them for 3–4 minutes over a medium heat until they are just pink.

Take the pan off the heat, swish in the salata, season to taste and serve immediately.

This is a lovely, fresh start to a meal, truly seasonal and full of bright, assertive flavours. The pear, needless to say, has to be totally ripe, juicy and sweet. Try to include oak leaf lettuce, rocket and watercress in the salad leaves – oak leaf for its colour; rocket and watercress for their bite.

autumn salad of figs and pear

100 g/4 oz mixed salad leaves

30 ml/2 tbsp hazelnut (filbert) oil

15 ml/1 tbsp fresh lemon juice

Sea salt and freshly ground black pepper

1 ripe pear, peeled and sliced

2 purple figs, quartered

15 g/½ oz/2 tbsp chopped, toasted hazelnuts

20 g/¾ oz Parmesan cheese shavings

Place the leaves in a salad bowl, sprinkle the oil, lemon juice and a little seasoning over and toss lightly.

Arrange it on two plates, top with the pear and figs, then the hazelnuts and finally the cheese shavings.

Serve at once.

We spent a week in Cefalù some years ago. We intended to make the lovely little Sicilian fishing port our base for exploring the northern half of the island and hired a car – which was a waste of money because we only managed to drag ourselves away from Cefalù for one day! Our apartment, on the top floor of a crumbling old building, was at one end of the beach, above the Piazza Garibaldi, and we spent most of our time on our terrace, with its breathtaking views across the Tyrrhenian Sea to Palermo; or wandering the narrow, cobblestone alleyways of the medieval quarter in search of yet another excellent restaurant; or sitting in the square below the Duomo sipping a glass of chilled prosecco and watching the world go by. So northern Sicily remained largely unexplored and must therefore be revisited.

These lovely crostini were served at all the bars and cafés and were a favourite lunch. They were topped with green olive paste – olivada – rather than tapenade but when I started experimenting on my return to my own kitchen, I found the sharpness of tapenade was even more delicious with the ham and cheese.

You will need about 30 g/1¼ oz of cheese but it's easier to buy a wedge and shave off as much as you want, keeping the rest for another time. Don't even think of using ready-grated Parmesan cheese!

parma ham, parmesan and tapenade crostini

6 thick slices of ciabatta

45 ml/3 tbsp olive oil

A wedge of Parmesan or Pecorino cheese

1 garlic clove, peeled

6 large slices of Parma ham

1 quantity of Green Olive and Oregano Tapenade (see page 18)

Preheat the oven to 200ºC/400ºF/gas 6/fan oven 180ºC.

Place the ciabatta slices on a baking (cookie) sheet lined with foil and brush the cut sides with the oil.

Bake for about 20 minutes until crisp and lightly golden.

While the bread is toasting, shave some long, thin slices from the cheese wedge with a vegetable peeler.

Rub the cut sides of the bread with the garlic clove.

Arrange a slice of ham on each piece of bread and top first with some tapenade and then the cheese shavings.

 Eat fairly soon after putting the crostini together, before they lose their wonderful texture.

smoked duck, asparagus and orange salad

450 g/1 lb asparagus, stems snapped off

2 large navel oranges

100 g/4 oz sliced smoked duck breast

60 ml/4 tbsp hazelnut (filbert) oil

Sea salt and freshly ground black pepper

2 long pieces of orange zest, to garnish (optional)

Bring a pan of salted water to a good rolling boil, add the asparagus and cook for about 4 minutes until just tender. Drain and set aside to cool.

Meanwhile, prepare the oranges. If you are intending to use the garnish, start off by stripping two long curls of zest by dragging the citrus zester around the orange from top to bottom. Then peel the oranges with a sharp knife over a bowl to reserve the juice. Remove the skin and pith, and segment the fruit by cutting along the inner membranes. Squeeze any remaining juice from the membranes into the bowl.

To assemble the salad, build up the asparagus spears on two plates in a random fashion, then arrange the orange segments and duck slices among and around them.

Make a dressing by whisking the oil with 90 ml/6 tbsp of the reserved orange juice. Season with salt and pepper and spoon over the salad.

Garnish with the orange zest curls, if using, and serve immediately.

This salad always fills me with nostalgia because it is so redolent of the Mediterranean: fragrant with herbs, sharp with yoghurt, crunchy with cucumber and onion, sweet with tomatoes – it makes me think of sun-drenched islands, balmy evenings and glittering turquoise seas.

mediterranean fattoush with greek yoghurt

2 wholemeal pitta breads

100 g/4 oz cherry tomatoes, quartered

35 g/1½ oz red onion, peeled and finely chopped

150 g/5 oz cucumber, halved lengthways and sliced into semi-circles

1 large garlic clove, peeled and crushed

15 g/½ oz fresh mint, coarsely chopped

15 g/½ oz fresh flatleaf parsley, coarsely chopped

100 ml/3½ fl oz/scant ½ cup extra virgin olive oil

Sea salt and freshly ground black pepper

120 ml/4 fl oz/½ cup Greek-style plain yoghurt

Preheat the oven to 150°C/300°F/gas 2/fan oven 135°C.

Cut the pitta breads into 2 cm/¾ in pieces. Lay them on a baking (cookie) sheet and bake in the oven for about 30 minutes until dry and crisp. Set aside to cool.

Place the tomatoes, onion, cucumber, garlic, herbs and three-quarters of the pitta bread in a roomy salad bowl.

Pour 75 ml/5 tbsp of the oil over, add some seasoning and mix gently. Spoon the yoghurt over the top – a stripy pattern looks nice – and season again.

Sprinkle the rest of the pitta bread pieces over the yoghurt and drizzle with the remaining olive oil.

Allow the salad to rest for about 20 minutes before serving so that the pitta bread can absorb some of the juices and soften.

 The bread can be baked up to 3 days ahead and kept in an airtight container.

leek, pear and bacon clafoutis

300 g/11 oz leeks

75 g/3 oz pancetta or smoked bacon rashers (slices), rinded

20 g/³/₄ oz butter

150 g/5 oz ripe pears

Sea salt and freshly ground black pepper

85 ml/3 fl oz/scant ¹/₃ cup double (heavy) cream

2 eggs

30 g/1¹/₄ oz freshly grated Parmesan cheese, plus extra for sprinkling

15 ml/1 tbsp chopped fresh parsley or snipped fresh chives

Preheat the oven to 200°C/400°F/gas 6/fan oven 180°C.

Trim the leeks by removing the root end and most of the green part – you should have about 200 g/7 oz left. Cut them lengthways almost down to the root and wash them well under cold running water. Shake out any excess water and slice into 1 cm/¹/₂ in pieces.

Cut the pancetta or bacon into strips. Melt the butter in a large frying pan, add the leeks and pancetta and cook over medium heat, stirring often, until they are soft and starting to brown.

Peel and core the pears and slice them into pieces about 1cm/¹/₂ in thick. Add to the frying pan and cook for a further 5 minutes. Season well and allow to cool slightly.

Whisk together the cream, eggs and cheese in a large bowl, and then stir in the pear and leek mixture. Transfer to a small gratin dish and cook in the oven for 30 minutes until firm and lightly browned.

Sprinkle with the parsley or chives and extra Parmesan and serve immediately.

Visit any part of northern Italy during the asparagus season and you will discover countless imaginative ways of cooking and serving it – more often than not roasted, which really concentrates the flavour. If you prefer, and the weather is good enough, the spears can be cooked on a barbecue. This gives them a slight smokiness that goes really well with this incredibly rich and indulgent sauce, which I learned many years ago from the owner of a skiing chalet in Courmayeur, where I worked for a winter season.

If you read the introduction, you'll already know that I recommend you use only local asparagus in season for the best flavour.

roasted asparagus parmigiana

70 g/3 oz smoked pancetta or bacon rashers (slices), rinded

75 ml/5 tbsp olive oil

1 large shallot (about 30 g/1¼ oz), peeled and finely chopped

2 garlic cloves, peeled and thinly sliced

200 ml/7 fl oz/scant 1 cup double (heavy) cream

125 g/4½ oz Mascarpone cheese

Sea salt and freshly ground black pepper

20 g/¾ oz/3 tbsp freshly grated Parmesan cheese

2–3 tbsp milk

75 g/3 oz/1½ cups soft brown breadcrumbs

15 g/½ oz/2 tbsp pine nuts

450 g/1 lb asparagus, stems snapped off

30 ml/2 tbsp snipped fresh chives

Preheat the oven to 230°C/450°F/gas 8/fan oven 210°C.

Grill (broil) the pancetta or bacon until crisp, place on some kitchen paper (paper towels) to drain and set aside to cool.

To make the sauce, heat 15 ml/1 tbsp of the oil in a small pan, add the shallot and garlic and cook for about 5 minutes until softened but not browned.

Add the cream and Mascarpone and bring to the boil over a gentle heat, stirring regularly.

Season to taste, add the Parmesan, and then crumble in two-thirds of the pancetta. Stir well. The sauce should have the consistency of thick cream; if it looks rather solid, add a little of the milk to thin it down.

Heat 30 ml/2 tbsp of the remaining oil in a small frying pan and add the breadcrumbs and pine nuts. Cook them over gentle heat, stirring often, until they are lightly browned and nicely crisp. Crumble in the remaining pancetta and set aside to cool.

Place the asparagus in an ovenproof dish and toss it with the remaining oil. Season with salt and pepper and roast for about 10 minutes until it just starts to brown at the edges.

To serve, place the asparagus on two warm plates. Reheat the sauce very briefly, spoon over the asparagus and top with the breadcrumb mixture and chives.

 The sauce can be prepared in advance to when the pancetta or bacon is added. Reheat it gently and thin with milk if necessary just before serving.

However unlikely the combination may sound, this is utterly delectable. We ate this *tapa* in Barcelona, where it was made with the wonderful Catalán black *butifarra* sausage. I managed to sneak some *butifarras* (along with fresh ceps and pickled anchovies) through Customs on my return, but of course they didn't sit for long in my refrigerator.

Butifarra, both black and white, being in short supply in my local provincial supermarket, I experimented with black pudding and was thrilled with the result.

king prawns with black pudding

45 ml/3 tbsp olive oil

2 garlic cloves, peeled and crushed

200 g/7 oz red onions, peeled and coarsely chopped

100 g/4 oz black pudding (blood sausage), cut into 1 cm/$^1/_2$ in thick slices

Sea salt and freshly ground black pepper

120 g/4$^1/_2$ oz raw prawns (shrimp), shelled and deveined

15 ml/1 tbsp chopped fresh parsley

Heat the oil in a heavy-based frying pan. Add the garlic and onion and cook for about 10 minutes, stirring occasionally, until they are soft and translucent.

Push them to the edge of the pan, add the black pudding slices and some seasoning and cook for about 4 minutes on each side.

Throw in the prawns (shrimp) and stir-fry everything just until the prawns turn pink.

Sprinkle with the parsley and serve immediately.

An easy sauce, positively sparkling with freshness and flavour, and a perfect foil for the richness of the mackerel. The bay leaves and orange permeate the flesh with a haunting aroma of citrus groves and southern market stalls festooned with great bunches of herbs. Dried bay leaves do not work in this recipe – they lack the green pungency of the fresh ones – so if you are not lucky enough to have a bay tree growing in a pot by your kitchen door, try using bushy sprigs of rosemary or thyme.

mackerel
with turkish almond sauce

75 g/3 oz/³/₄ cup almonds, skinned

100 ml/3¹/₂ fl oz/scant ¹/₂ cup olive oil

2 mackerel, cleaned

1 large orange

4 fresh bay leaves

15 ml/1 tbsp capers, rinsed, squeezed dry and coarsely chopped

5 ml/1 tsp cider vinegar or wine vinegar

6 anchovy fillets, finely chopped

Sea salt and freshly ground black pepper

30 ml/2 tbsp fresh mint, coarsely chopped

Heat the oven to 160°C/325°F/gas 3/fan oven 145°C.

Place the almonds on a baking (cookie) sheet and cook them for 20 minutes until deeply golden. Allow to cool slightly, then chop coarsely.

Increase the oven heat to 200°C/400°F/gas 6/fan oven 180°C. Brush a roasting tin with a little of the oil and place the mackerel in it. Halve the orange, then cut two whole slices from it. Cut these slices in half and place them and the bay leaves inside the mackerel. Bake the mackerel for 20 minutes.

Meanwhile, assemble the sauce. Squeeze the orange juice from the rest of the orange and place it in a small bowl with the capers, vinegar, anchovies and some seasoning. Slowly whisk in the remaining oil using a wire whisk – it will thicken as you go – then add the almonds and mint.

Place the mackerel on two warm plates and pour the almond sauce over.

 You can use toasted flaked (slivered) almonds if you prefer, although they will not give you quite the same crunch and texture; somehow whole toasted almonds have a much mellower, deeper flavour.

I tend to thread scallops on to a flat metal skewer before cooking because it makes them so much easier to turn. They need a very short cooking time to preserve their lovely texture and sweet, delicate flavour, and if you are chasing them all around the frying pan trying to flip them over with a spatula, chances are you will end up with very expensive rubber.

Chermoula is a gloriously fragrant Moroccan mix of spices and herbs that can be used as a marinade, a sauce or a salad dressing.

scallops in smoked salmon with beans and chermoula

100 g/4 oz smoked salmon

6 scallops without roe

15 ml/1 tbsp olive oil

FOR THE PURÉE:

1 x 400 g/14 oz/large can of haricot (navy) beans, rinsed and drained

1 garlic clove, peeled

50 ml/2 fl oz olive oil

Sea salt and freshly ground black pepper

Juice of 1 lemon

FOR THE CHERMOULA:

15 g/$^1/_2$ oz fresh parsley

15 g/$^1/_2$ oz fresh coriander (cilantro)

5 ml/1 tsp cumin seeds, coarsely ground

2.5 ml/$^1/_2$ tsp sweet paprika

A pinch of cayenne pepper

150 ml/$^1/_4$ pint/$^2/_3$ cup olive oil

Juice of $^1/_2$ lemon

Sea salt and freshly ground black pepper

To make the purée, place the beans, garlic, oil and some seasoning in a food processor and process until fairly smooth. Add enough of the lemon juice to bring out and sharpen the flavour – start off with $\frac{1}{2}$ tbsp and add more if necessary.

Place the purée in a glass or china bowl and heat it over a pan of boiling water or in a microwave. Rinse out the food processor.

To make the chermoula, place all the ingredients in the food processor and process until smooth.

Cut the smoked salmon into strips about $1\frac{1}{2}$ cm/$^2/_3$ in wide and wrap them around the scallops. Carefully thread three wrapped scallops on to a flat metal skewer. Repeat with the remaining scallops.

Heat the oil in a frying pan over medium heat until really hot and cook the scallops for about 1 minute on each side. Remove the pan from the heat and pour the chermoula over the scallops – the residual heat will enhance the fragrance even more.

To serve, divide the purée between two warm plates, top with the scallops and drizzle the chermoula over and around them.

Fish cooked on the bone always seems to be so much moister and more flavoursome than fillets, and monkfish lends itself to this perfectly as it is easy to divide into two fillets once cooked.

The Mexican-inspired marinade is bright and zesty, more than a match for the rich and lively avocado salsa.

spiced fillet of monkfish with guacamole

500 g monkfish tail, skinned

FOR THE MARINADE:

1 garlic clove, peeled and crushed

50 g/2 oz red onion, peeled and thinly sliced

Juice and grated zest of 1 orange

Grated zest of 1 lemon

15 ml/1 tbsp fresh lemon juice

5 ml/1 tsp cumin seeds, coarsely ground

5 ml/1 tsp coriander (cilantro) seeds, coarsely ground

10 black olives, stoned (pitted) and halved

60 ml/4 tbsp olive oil

15 g/$\frac{1}{2}$ oz fresh flatleaf parsley, coarsely chopped

15 g/$\frac{1}{2}$ oz fresh coriander, coarsely chopped

FOR THE GUACAMOLE:

1 large, ripe avocado

1 garlic clove, peeled

25 g/1 oz red onion, peeled and coarsely chopped

5 ml/1 tsp lemon juice

30 ml/2 tbsp olive oil

Sea salt and freshly ground black pepper

75 g/3 oz cherry tomatoes, quartered

15 g/$\frac{1}{2}$ oz fresh coriander, plus extra for garnish

To make the marinade, mix together all the ingredients in an ovenproof china dish. Add the monkfish and spoon the marinade over it. Set aside for at least 30 minutes, turning it over once.

To make the guacamole, place all the ingredients except the tomatoes and coriander in a food processor and process until smooth. Check the seasoning and add a little more lemon juice if it needs sharpening.

Scrape the guacamole into a bowl, stir in the tomatoes and garnish with the coriander leaves. Set aside while you cook the monkfish.

Preheat the oven to 200°C/400°F/gas 6/fan oven 180°C.

Cook the monkfish for 20 minutes, basting it with the juices half-way through. Remove from the oven and allow to rest for 5 minutes, then run a sharp knife along each side of the bone to divide it into two fillets.

Place the fillets on two warm plates, spoon the juices over and serve immediately with the guacamole.

 It is better not to make the guacamole too far ahead of time as it will lose its fabulous colour.

We spent a fortnight exploring Apulia, in southern Italy, many years ago, when it was still relatively undiscovered. The little fishing port of Trani was our first base, and we were entranced by the freshness of the seafood, and by our first experience of focaccia and sun-dried tomatoes. We came across different versions of these prawns throughout our trip – as a fish course, a pasta sauce, an antipasto, a topping for pizza, even a filling for calzone – and we were always informed with great pride that the restaurant dried its own tomatoes.

apulian prawns with sun-dried tomatoes

20 g/³/₄ oz/3 tbsp pine nuts

150 g/5 oz thin French (green) beans

60 ml/4 tbsp extra virgin olive oil

200 g/7 oz raw king prawns (shrimp), shelled and deveined

1 x 400 g/14 oz/large can of haricot (navy) beans, rinsed and drained

4 spring onions (scallions), thinly sliced

2 garlic cloves, peeled and crushed

30 ml/2 tbsp capers, rinsed and squeezed dry

14 black olives, stoned (pitted) and halved

6 sun-dried tomato halves, cut into strips

20 g/³/₄ oz/3 tbsp freshly grated Parmesan cheese

Sea salt and freshly ground black pepper

15 g/¹/₂ oz chopped fresh parsley

Place the pine nuts in a small ovenproof dish and bake them in a preheated oven at 150°C/300°F/gas 2/fan oven 135°C for 20 minutes until lightly golden.

Top and tail the French beans, cut them in half and cook in salted boiling water for 5 minutes until just tender. Drain, cool under cold running water and set aside.

Heat the oil in a large frying pan and add the prawns and haricot beans. Cook over a medium heat for about 5 minutes, stirring all the time, until the prawns just turn pink.

Stir in all the remaining ingredients except the parsley and heat through for a couple of minutes.

Check the seasoning, sprinkle with the parsley and serve.

Tahini, a paste made of sesame seeds, is a popular ingredient throughout the Middle East. Its flavour can be elusive when combined with bolder, more aggressive partners, but that is one of its strengths in my opinion, as its rich, toasty nuttiness is a whisper, a promise – but never a statement.

stir-fried chicken in tahini sauce

30 ml/2 tbsp olive oil

150 g/5 oz red onion, peeled and sliced

2 garlic cloves, peeled and crushed

1 large red (bell) pepper, about 200 g/7 oz, seeded and cut into 3 cm/1¼ in long strips

150 g/5 oz sugar snap peas

85 ml/3 fl oz/scant ⅓ cup dark tahini

150 ml/¼ pint/⅔ cup Greek-style plain yoghurt

2 chicken supremes

Sea salt and freshly ground black pepper

30 ml/2 tbsp chopped fresh coriander (cilantro)

50 g/2 oz/½ cup shelled salted pistachio nuts

Heat the oil in a large frying pan or wok, add the onion, garlic and pepper strips and cook over medium heat for about 15 minutes until soft.

Meanwhile, cook the sugar snap peas in plenty of salted boiling water for 3 minutes. Drain and cool under cold running water.

Whisk together the tahini and yoghurt in a small bowl.

Turn up the heat under the frying pan, add the chicken and stir-fry until firm and just starting to brown. Add the sugar snaps and cook for a further 1 minute, then stir in the tahini and yoghurt mixture and some seasoning. Cook for just long enough to heat the sauce but do not bring it to the boil – just get it nice and steaming.

Stir in the coriander and pistachios and serve immediately.

spice-rubbed chicken with fruit and nut couscous

Couscous is a real boon when you are in a hurry as it is precooked and all you have to do is rehydrate it, making it much more convenient than any of the whole grains. It also absorbs other flavours easily – olive oil, lemon juice, vinegar, herbs, stock, spices. Always be sure to fluff up couscous with a fork once or twice while it is rehydrating and before serving to give it a wonderful lightness.

15 ml/1 tbsp olive oil

2.5 ml/$\frac{1}{2}$ tsp dried oregano

2.5 ml/$\frac{1}{2}$ tsp garam masala

5 ml/1 tsp lemon juice

Sea salt and freshly ground black pepper

2 chicken supremes

FOR THE YOGHURT:

250 ml/8 fl oz/1 cup Greek-style plain yoghurt

1 red chilli, seeded and sliced

1 garlic clove, peeled and crushed

15 g/$\frac{1}{2}$ oz fresh mint, coarsely chopped

2 spring onions (scallions), finely sliced

Sea salt and freshly ground black pepper

FOR THE COUSCOUS:

300 ml/$\frac{1}{2}$ pint/1$\frac{1}{4}$ cups water

100 g/4 oz couscous

25 g/1 oz dried apricots, cut into strips

25 g/1 oz raisins

4 sun-dried tomato halves, cut into strips

15 ml/1 tbsp capers, rinsed and squeezed dry

1 heaped tsp bouillon powder

Sea salt and freshly ground black pepper

25 g/1 oz/$\frac{1}{4}$ cup dry-roasted peanuts

Mix together the oil, oregano, garam masala, lemon juice and seasoning in a ramekin (custard cup).

Line a grill (broiler) pan with foil, place the chicken supremes on it and rub the spice mix into them. Leave to marinate for at least 30 minutes (an hour is better).

Preheat the grill (broiler) to high and cook the chicken, about 3 cm/1¼ in from the heat, for 5 minutes on each side. Set aside to rest for about 10 minutes before slicing.

Mix together all the ingredients for the yoghurt, adding seasoning to taste.

Bring the water for the couscous to the boil in a pan and add all the couscous ingredients except the peanuts. Give it a stir, remove from the heat, cover and put aside for 5 minutes to steam.

Fluff up the couscous with a fork, re-cover and allow to steam for a further 5 minutes. Then fluff it up again, mix in the peanuts and check the seasoning.

To serve, slice the chicken supremes and place them on warm plates with a spoonful of couscous and a dollop of the yoghurt.

Sweet, spicy, savoury and herby – this pesto is a perfect partner for rich duck. I never remove the skin from duck breasts, as I love its flavour – smearing it with a bit of honey and sprinkling it with salt before cooking gives it a delicious caramelised crispness which is irresistible. You can give a whole duck the same treatment, rubbing it all over with honey and salt before roasting; it will come out of the oven burnished and bronzed to perfection.

grilled duck with mango and basil pesto

15 ml/1 tbsp vegetable oil

2 duck breast fillets, about 200 g/7 oz each

10 ml/2 tsp runny honey

15 ml/1 tbsp sea salt flakes (not crystals)

FOR THE PESTO:

20 g/³/₄ oz fresh basil leaves

1 garlic clove, peeled

20 g/³/₄ oz/3 tbsp freshly grated Parmesan cheese

150 ml/¹/₄ pint/²/₃ cup olive oil

Juice of ¹/₂ lime

Sea salt and freshly ground black pepper

1 small mango, peeled and diced

1 red chilli, seeded and finely sliced

Heat the vegetable oil in a frying pan. Add the duck, flesh-side down, and brown over a high heat for 2–3 minutes to seal.

Preheat the grill (broiler) to high. Transfer the duck to a roasting tray, skin-side up, spread the honey over the skin, then sprinkle with the salt.

Grill (broil) about 8 cm/3 in below the heat for 4–5 minutes until the skin is crisp and dark. Remove from the grill, cover loosely with a piece of foil and leave to rest for 10 minutes before carving.

While the duck is resting, to make the pesto place all the ingredients except the mango and chilli in a food processor and process until fairly smooth. Scrape into a bowl and gently mix in the mango and chilli.

Slice the duck thinly and serve with the pesto.

Rhubarb without sugar is mouth-puckeringly inedible, but add some sweetness to it and it offers true versatility, a wonderful balance of sweet and sour that works equally well in savoury dishes and puddings. The ginger gives this sauce another layer of flavour, a hint of spice and caramel and warm fruit.

Make sure that you buy brightly coloured rhubarb – as close to magenta and Mexican pink as possible – or your sauce with have a grey tinge to it.

If you have any sauce left over, add a little more sugar or some honey to it and have it with Greek-style yoghurt for breakfast!

pork fillet with rhubarb and ginger sauce

200 g/7 oz rhubarb

40 g/1½ oz caster (superfine) sugar

15 ml/1 tbsp olive oil

Sea salt and freshly ground black pepper

1 small pork fillet, about 350 g/12 oz

A knob of stem ginger in syrup, finely chopped

15 ml/1 tbsp ginger syrup from the jar

Preheat the oven to 200°C/400°F/gas 6/fan oven 180°C.

Wash and dry the rhubarb and cut it into 2 cm/¾ in lengths. Place in a china or glass ovenproof dish, sprinkle with the sugar and bake uncovered for 20 minutes – it will stew nicely in its own juices.

Remove the rhubarb from the oven (leave the oven on) and allow to cool while the pork is cooking.

Heat the oil in a heavy-based frying pan. Season the pork fillet and brown it all over in the hot oil. Transfer to a roasting tin and roast in the oven for 15 minutes.

Turn off the oven, leave the door ajar, and allow the pork to rest for 10 minutes before slicing.

Transfer the rhubarb to a food processor and blend until smooth. Stir in the ginger and syrup.

Carve the pork fillet into 1 cm/½ in slices and serve with the sauce.

Some years ago, towards the end of my professional catering career, I was asked to provide the food for a barbecue. My client was a major German bank with offices in the City of London – in a 22-storey building with a roof garden overlooking the Thames. The menu was to be utterly simple: chicken drumsticks, sausages and hamburgers. It was the hamburgers that induced my faint feeling of panic, for the simple reason that I had never actually made a hamburger!

After much feverish experimenting, I came up with my own definitive hamburger recipe and I eventually found myself making 900 hamburgers – by hand! I made them in batches of 20 and they took me 3 days. First I made the mix, which I then patted into a pastry ring to shape it into hamburgers; these I placed on a baking (cookie) sheet. Finally they went into the large hired freezer that was humming away in my dining room. Then I started the whole process again. And again. And again. Hamburger hell!

They caused an absolute sensation at the party and I realised from the guests' comments that they had never eaten a home-made hamburger before. And yet they are in fact so easy to make – at least in small quantities!

home-made hamburgers with red onion

makes four good-sized hamburgers

50 g/2 oz wholemeal bread

250 g/9 oz red onion, peeled and roughly chopped

15 g/½ oz fresh parsley, roughly chopped

30 ml/2 tbsp Worcestershire sauce

500 g/18 oz lean minced (ground) beef or lamb

5 ml/1 tsp sea salt

Freshly ground black pepper

4 hamburger buns

Place the bread, onion and parsley in a food processor and process until finely chopped.

Scrape it all into a large bowl, add the Worcestershire sauce, meat and seasoning and mix well with your hands – messy but fun! Shape into four patties, place on a plate or baking (cookie) sheet, and chill for 30 minutes to firm up.

Cook on a barbecue, on a ridged cast-iron grill (broiler) pan or under a grill for about 3 minutes on each side, so that they are nice and brown on the outside but juicy and slightly rare in the middle.

Split the hamburger buns, place a burger in each and serve.

 Serve in the hamburger buns with mustard, ketchup or whatever you fancy. The Provençal Roasted Red Pepper Aioli on page 64 is wonderful with them!

A good steak, properly cooked, needs little embellishment, but I do love this sauce with it. Tarragon is a time-honoured partner for beef but, while the classic sauce béarnaise is rich and heavy, this sauce is fresh, tangy and herby and works a treat. It is mayonnaise-based and lightened with yoghurt. You can eat it immediately if you are short of time, but the flavour develops very well if left for an hour or so.

steak with rocket and tarragon sauce

1 egg yolk

80 ml/2½ fl oz/scant ⅓ cup olive oil, plus extra for brushing

80 ml/2½ fl oz/scant ⅓ cup Greek-style plain yoghurt

1 garlic clove, peeled

15 g/½ oz red onion, coarsely chopped

40 g/1½ oz rocket leaves

20 g/¾ oz fresh tarragon, stalks removed

Sea salt and freshly ground black pepper

A squeeze of lemon juice (optional)

2 steaks

Sea salt and freshly ground black pepper

Place the egg yolk in a small bowl and whisk it with an electric beater. Slowly whisk in the oil to make a thick, glossy mayonnaise.

Scrape the mixture into a food processor and add the yoghurt, garlic, onion, rocket and tarragon. Process until fairly smooth – it will go a beautiful pistachio green.

Add seasoning to taste, and the lemon juice if it does not have quite enough bite for your liking. Set aside until you are ready to eat.

When you are ready to cook the steaks, brush them with oil, season them well, and fry them in a really hot frying pan or ridged cast-iron grill pan. I like my steak underdone so I give it only about 3 minutes on each side.

Serve with the sauce.

 The sauce will keep in the fridge for 24 hours – but allow time to bring it back to room temperature before using it.

These herb- and spice-scented koftas could be Mexican, Middle Eastern or Indian! The flavouring fits happily into all three cuisines, so if you would rather use tortillas or naan than pitta breads, do not hesitate. And, of course, if you fancy cooking them on a barbecue they will taste even better.

Mango is my favourite fruit for the raita, but pineapple, pomegranate or fig are just as delicious.

lamb koftas with fruit raita

FOR THE KOFTAS:

75 g/3 oz red onion, peeled and coarsely chopped

1 large garlic clove, peeled

1 red chilli, halved and seeded

5 ml/1 tsp cumin seeds, coarsely ground

5 ml/1 tsp coriander (cilantro) seeds, coarsely ground

20 g/³/₄ oz fresh coriander

15 g/¹/₂ oz fresh parsley

5 ml/1 tsp sea salt

Freshly ground black pepper

350 g/12 oz minced (ground) lamb

4 pitta breads

FOR THE RAITA:

1 small, ripe mango, peeled and diced

40 g/1³/₄ oz red onion, peeled and finely chopped

1 small red chilli, seeded and finely chopped

30 ml/2 tbsp olive oil

250 ml/8 fl oz/1 cup Greek-style plain yoghurt

15 g/¹/₂ oz fresh coriander, roughly chopped

Sea salt and freshly ground black pepper

Place all the ingredients for the kofta except the lamb and pitta breads in a food processor and pulse until finely chopped.

Scrape it into a bowl, add the lamb and mix thoroughly – the best way to do this is with your hands and it's delightfully messy!

Divide the mixture into four and shape it round four flat metal skewers. Place on a foil-lined baking (cookie) sheet.

Mix together all the raita ingredients in a small bowl and stir well.

Heat the grill (broiler) to high. Grill (broil) the koftas 10 cm/4 in from the heat for 5 minutes on each side. Serve immediately with the pitta bread and raita.

This dish is packed with fresh, clean summer flavours, sharp and aromatic, with mint playing its traditional role as a partner to lamb in the couscous and the Italian-inspired sauce. A mixture of red and yellow cherry tomatoes looks really pretty. Fillet of lamb is expensive but well flavoured and beautifully tender; it requires very little cooking, just a quick seal in a hot frying pan and a brief blast in a hot oven, making it ideal for Quickstep days.

The strength of the sauce will depend on how potent the herbs are, and this type of dish should certainly have plenty of bite. However, if you would prefer a more delicately flavoured sauce, add one anchovy, then taste before adding the second.

roast fillet of lamb with warm minted couscous salad

A little olive oil, for browning

1 lamb fillet, trimmed of fat, about 250 g/9 oz

FOR THE MINT SAUCE:

1 garlic clove, peeled

20 g/³/₄ oz fresh mint

15 ml/1 tbsp capers, rinsed and squeezed dry

150 ml/¹/₄ pint/²/₃ cup olive oil

2 anchovy fillets

20 g/³/₄ oz/3 tbsp freshly grated Parmesan cheese

A squeeze of lemon juice (optional)

FOR THE COUSCOUS:

250 ml/8 fl oz/1 cup water

90 g/3¹/₂ oz couscous

1 heaped tsp bouillon powder

Sea salt and freshly ground black pepper

25 g/1 oz red onion, peeled and finely chopped

1 garlic clove, peeled and crushed

125 g/4¹/₂ oz cherry tomatoes, quartered

1 piece of Lemon Pickled in Salt and Lemon Juice (see page 19), finely chopped

30 ml/2 tbsp olive oil, plus extra for browning

15 g/¹/₂ oz fresh mint, coarsely chopped

Start with the sauce as it will sit happily for half an hour, although any longer than that and it will lose its bright green colour (but not its flavour!). Place all the ingredients except the lemon juice in a food processor and process until smooth. Set aside until you are ready to eat.

Preheat the oven to 200°C/400°F/gas 6/fan oven 180°C.

Heat a heavy-based frying pan over high heat, add a little oil and brown the lamb briefly on all sides to seal it. Transfer it to a roasting tin and roast in the oven for 5–10 minutes, depending on the thickness of the lamb, until just cooked but still pink in the centre. Turn off the oven, open the door and leave the lamb to rest in the oven until you are ready to carve.

Bring the water for the couscous to the boil, then turn off the heat and stir in the couscous, bouillon powder and some seasoning. Cover and leave to rest for 5 minutes.

Fluff up the couscous with a fork and carefully fold in all the remaining couscous ingredients except the mint. Cover and leave to rest for a further 5 minutes, then check the seasoning and fold in the mint.

Check the mint sauce seasoning and add some lemon juice if it needs sharpening.

Carve the lamb into 5 mm/¼ in slices. Divide the couscous between two warm plates, top with the lamb and serve immediately with the mint sauce.

venison steaks with black plums

30 ml/2 tbsp olive oil

125 g/4¹/₂ oz red onion, peeled and coarsely chopped

1.5 ml/¹/₄ tsp ground cinnamon

150 g/5 oz black plums, stoned (pitted) and quartered

120 ml/4 fl oz/¹/₂ cup port

Sea salt and freshly ground black pepper

A squeeze of lemon juice (optional)

2 venison steaks, cut from the loin

15 ml/1 tbsp chopped fresh parsley

1 bunch of watercress

Heat half the oil in a small saucepan, add the onion and cook over a gentle heat, stirring occasionally, for about 15 minutes until soft.

Stir in the cinnamon and plums, cover and simmer for 20 minutes until the plums have broken down.

Add the port, bring to the boil and cook, covered, for a further 15 minutes.

Allow to cool slightly, then scrape into a food processor and process until smooth. Return to the saucepan, season and heat gently. Taste and sharpen with the lemon juice if necessary – it will depend on the sweetness of the plums.

Season the venison well. Heat the remaining oil in a frying pan and cook the steaks over a medium to high heat for about 4 minutes on each side for pink, a bit longer if you want them well done. Remove from the heat and allow the meat to rest for 5 minutes.

Place on two warm plates, sprinkle with the parsley, garnish with the watercress and serve with the sauce.

The fragrance that wafts from the pan as the pesto comes into contact with the hot noodles and vegetables is mesmerising. The flavours in this dish are unmistakably Eastern so I sometimes substitute traditional Japanese noodles, such as udon, and strips of smoked salmon or smoked tuna instead of the bacon.

egg noodles with coriander, cashew and coconut pesto

30 ml/2 tbsp toasted sesame oil

100 g/4 oz smoked bacon rashers (slices), rinded and chopped

125 g/4½ oz red onion, peeled and sliced

1 garlic clove, peeled and crushed

1 large red or yellow (bell) pepper, about 200 g/7 oz, seeded and cut into 1 cm/½ in wide strips

250 g/9 oz egg noodles

75 g/3 oz frozen peas

1 quantity of Coriander, Cashew and Coconut Pesto (see page 17)

Sea salt and freshly ground black pepper

Heat the oil in a frying pan and add the bacon. Brown for 5 minutes, then add the onion, garlic and pepper strips. Cook for 10–15 minutes, stirring occasionally.

Cook the noodles in plenty of salted boiling water according to the manufacturer's instructions, adding the peas towards the end of the cooking time just to heat them. Drain it all well and return to the saucepan. Stir in the pepper and onion mixture, then the pesto.

Season to taste and serve immediately.

 For a vegetarian version, try replacing the bacon with baby sweetcorn or water chestnuts.

penne with tomatoes, feta and green lentils

This is one of those incredibly comforting dishes, easy to make, easy to eat, honest and satisfying – food for a cold blustery night, or for when you are tired and out of sorts. I always feel soothed and reassured when I cook it! Feta is not a common partner for pasta but, as it melts into the sauce, it gives it a deep, savoury richness and a faint sharpness that accentuates the earthiness of the lentils and penne.

30 ml/2 tbsp olive oil

200 g/7 oz onions, peeled and sliced

1 garlic clove, peeled and crushed

1 x 400 g/14 oz/large can of chopped tomatoes

85 g/3 oz/$\frac{1}{2}$ cup green lentils

100 ml/3$\frac{1}{2}$ fl oz/scant $\frac{1}{2}$ cup water

Sea salt and freshly ground black pepper

250 g/9 oz wholemeal penne

100 g/4 oz /1 cup Feta cheese, crumbled

30 ml/2 tbsp chopped fresh parsley

Heat the oil in a large saucepan. Add the onions and garlic and cook over medium heat for 10 minutes until starting to brown.

Stir in the tomatoes and lentils. Add the water, bring to the boil, cover and simmer for 30 minutes, stirring occasionally. Season to taste.

Cook the penne in salted boiling water for 15 minutes. Drain and add to the tomato and lentil sauce.

Check the seasoning, stir in the cheese, sprinkle with the parsley and serve.

The Cretans use dried broad beans – *yahní* – for this purée; it is thick and earthy, nourishes the soul just as much as the body, and provides a splendid foil to the sharp, fresh, aromatic salata. We ate it often during a walking holiday in Crete, at small, family-run, out-of-the way restaurants that served traditional food. I have tried making it with dried split yellow peas as well, but luckily red lentils work very well and cook much faster.

cretan lentil purée with greek salata

30 ml/2 tbsp olive oil

250 g/9 oz onions, peeled and coarsely chopped

2 garlic cloves, peeled and crushed

175 g/6 oz/1 cup red lentils

500 ml/17 fl oz/2¼ cups chicken or vegetable stock – bouillon powder will do

1 bay leaf

Sea salt and freshly ground black pepper

1 quantity of Greek Salata with Fresh Herbs (see page 20)

Heat the oil in a medium-sized heavy-based saucepan. Add the onion and garlic and cook gently, stirring occasionally, for about 20 minutes until soft and golden.

Add the lentils, stock and bay leaf and bring to the boil. Reduce the heat to low, cover and simmer gently for 20–30 minutes, stirring occasionally, until the lentils are soft and thick.

Season with salt and pepper and divide between two large shallow bowls. Spoon the salata on top and serve immediately.

coriander lentils with lemon grass, garlic and ginger

Spiked with lemon grass, chilli, garlic and ginger, and mellow with coconut and sesame oil, these lentils are worth making just for the glorious aromas that seep tantalisingly from the pan! The chillies need to be on the hot side or they will not be able to stand up to the coconut.

FOR THE LENTILS:

3 stalks of lemon grass, papery outer skins discarded, finely sliced

4 garlic cloves, peeled

A knob of fresh root ginger, about 40 g/1^2/$_3$ oz, peeled and coarsely chopped

100 g/4 oz red onions, peeled and coarsely chopped

2 hottish green chillies, seeded and coarsely chopped

30 ml/2 tbsp toasted sesame oil

400 ml/14 fl oz/1^3/$_4$ cups coconut milk

350 ml/12 fl oz/1^1/$_3$ cups water

250 g/9 oz/1^1/$_2$ cups Puy lentils

Juice of 1 lime

50 g/2 oz creamed coconut, coarsely chopped

FOR THE TOPPING:

15 ml/1 tbsp coriander (cilantro) seeds

45 ml/3 tbsp toasted sesame oil

250 g/9 oz red onions, peeled and cut into ^{1}/$_2$ cm/^{1}/$_4$ in thick slices

Sea salt and freshly ground black pepper

20 g/^{3}/$_4$ oz fresh coriander, very coarsely chopped

To make the lentils, place the lemon grass, garlic, ginger, onions and chillies in a food processor and process until very finely chopped.

Heat the oil in a heavy-based saucepan over a medium heat, add the chopped vegetables and cook gently, stirring frequently, for about 10 minutes without browning.

Stir in the coconut milk and water and bring to the boil.

Add the lentils, turn the heat right down, cover and leave to simmer for about 40 minutes until the lentils are tender and the liquid well reduced and aromatic.

Meanwhle, to make the topping, toast the coriander seeds in a small heavy-based saucepan until fragrant. Transfer them to a mortar or electric spice grinder and grind them coarsely.

Heat the oil in a small frying pan and stir in the coriander seeds, onions and some seasoning. Fry gently, stirring occasionally, until the onions are soft and translucent – do not let them brown.

When the lentils are ready, stir in the lime juice and creamed coconut and continue to cook until the coconut has melted. Add the chopped coriander to the topping mixture. Check the seasoning and serve the lentils topped with the coriander onions.

spaghetti with pickled lemons, olives, tomatoes and parmesan

Although the tomatoes take time to roast, this is an incredibly easy recipe, full of bright, Mediterranean flavours. Do grate the Parmesan cheese yourself in a food processor, as the ready-grated stuff in a tub would contribute little to the taste and give it a powdery texture rather than a chewy, melted cheese richness.

250 g/9 oz tomatoes, quartered

Sea salt and freshly ground black pepper

60 ml/4 tbsp olive oil

15 ml/1 tbsp runny honey

300 g/11 oz wholemeal spaghetti

12 black olives, stoned (pitted) and halved

2 pieces of Lemon Pickled in Salt and Lemon Juice (see page 19), finely chopped

100 g/4 oz/1 cup freshly grated Parmesan cheese

30 ml/2 tbsp chopped fresh parsley

Preheat the oven to 200°C/400°F/gas 6/fan oven 180°C.

Place the tomatoes, cut-sides up, on a baking (cookie) sheet lined with foil, season well, and drizzle first with half of the oil and then with the honey. Roast for 45 minutes until the tomatoes are soft and blackened slightly along the edges.

When the tomatoes are nearly ready, cook the spaghetti in plenty of salted boiling water for 10 minutes, drain and return to the saucepan.

Add some seasoning to the spaghetti, the remaining oil, the olives, pickled lemon and Parmesan. Mix well, then gently fold in the tomatoes and the parsley.

Serve immediately.

We already knew from eating our way through the Périgord years ago that goose fat and potatoes had a tremendous affinity for each other, but it was not until we came across a similar dish in the Languedoc more recently that we discovered a marriage made in heaven: add some whole, unpeeled garlic cloves and a handful of the herbs that grow wild in the sun-baked hills and you end up with a dish that is so savoury, aromatic and satisfying as to constitute ultimate gratification! It's so good that it doesn't actually need any accompaniment; we often have it on its own for supper with a salad.

It may seem like a lot of potatoes, but they are so moreish that, if you cook any less, you will feel cheated and you will argue over which of you gets to scrape out the pan. Don't peel the potatoes as the skin acquires a wonderful texture, and be sure to stay in the kitchen while they are cooking because the aroma emanating from the oven is hypnotic!

garlicky potatoes roasted in goose fat

500 g/18 oz red potatoes, scrubbed and cut into chunks

2 bay leaves

A handful of pungent, aromatic herbs such as rosemary, oregano or thyme

30 ml/2 tbsp goose fat (available in delicatessens and some supermarkets)

Sea salt and freshly ground black pepper

At least 20 whole, unpeeled garlic cloves

Preheat the oven to 200°C/400°F/gas 6/fan oven 180°C.

Boil the potatoes in plenty of salted water for 5 minutes. Drain and return to the saucepan, cover with a lid and give them a good shake to rough up the surfaces.

Tip the potatoes into a large roasting tin and add the herbs, goose fat and some seasoning. Toss it all together with a large spoon, then roast for 45 minutes, stirring once after 30 minutes.

Add the garlic cloves and cook for a further 30 minutes, stirring once or twice.

Serve immediately.

 Duck fat works just as well as goose fat in this dish.

Cauliflower cheese can be heaven or hell – a rich, golden, savoury swan or a drab, watery, mushy ugly duckling. This is a very simple but infinitely better version than the old-fashioned white-sauced one, decidedly rich and golden, good and cheesy, and quick to make into the bargain!

rich and golden cauliflower cheese

1 medium cauliflower, broken into florets

200 ml/7 fl oz/scant 1 cup double (heavy) cream

Sea salt and freshly ground black pepper

75 g/3 oz/³/₄ cup freshly grated Parmesan cheese

Pre-heat the oven to 200°C/400°F/gas 6/fan oven 180°C.

Steam the cauliflower florets for about 10 minutes until they are just cooked but still have a bit of crunch to them.

Transfer the florets to an ovenproof dish and pour the cream over. Season well and sprinkle with the cheese.

Bake for about 40 minutes until the cream is bubbling and golden. Serve immediately.

warm mango and pineapple in butterscotch and port sauce

50 g/2 oz/$\frac{1}{4}$ cup light brown sugar

120 ml/4 fl oz/$\frac{1}{2}$ cup ruby port

120 ml/4 fl oz/$\frac{1}{2}$ cup freshly squeezed orange juice (about 2 oranges)

120 ml/4 fl oz/$\frac{1}{2}$ cup double (heavy) cream

1 ripe mango, peeled and cut into 1 cm/$\frac{1}{2}$ in chunks

1 baby pineapple, peeled and cut into 1 cm/$\frac{1}{2}$ in chunks

30 g/1 oz/$\frac{1}{4}$ cup flaked (slivered) toasted almonds

Place the sugar, port and orange juice in a frying pan. Stir to dissolve the sugar, bring to the boil and simmer for 15 minutes until reduced by half.

Add the cream and cook for a further 5 minutes to thicken. Stir in the fruit, bring back to the boil and immediately remove from the heat.

Sprinkle with the almonds and serve.

pear, chocolate and caramel crisps

20 g/³/₄ oz butter

50 g/2 oz/¹/₄ cup caster (superfine) sugar

2 ripe, juicy pears, peeled, cored and sliced

40 g/1³/₄ oz dark chocolate (52% minimum cocoa solids), coarsely chopped

FOR THE TOPPING:

50 g/2 oz/¹/₄ cup unsalted (sweet) butter

20 g/³/₄ oz dark brown sugar

20 g/³/₄ oz caster (superfine) sugar

25 g/1 oz/¹/₄ cup plain (all-purpose) white flour

25 g/1 oz/¹/₄ cup wholemeal flour

15 g/¹/₂ oz/2 tbsp chopped, toasted hazelnuts (filberts)

TO SERVE:

Double (heavy) cream

Melt the butter in a small heavy-based saucepan, stir in the sugar and cook over a medium heat until the mixture caramelises and turns golden – watch it carefully as it will burn easily.

Pour the caramel immediately into two individual gratin dishes, about 13 cm/ 5 in diameter. Allow to cool.

Preheat the oven to 200°C/400°F/gas 6/fan oven 180°C.

To make the topping, place all the ingredients except the hazelnuts in a food processor and process until the mixture resembles coarse breadcrumbs. Stir in the nuts.

Place the pears and chocolate on top of the caramel, spoon the topping evenly over and bake for 10–15 minutes until the topping is golden.

Allow to cool slightly before serving as the caramel will be very, very hot!

You need individual gratin dishes for this recipe. I find them really useful when cooking for two so once you have some, you'll wonder how you managed without them.

This is such an easy pudding, which I make with the same orange butter as I use for crêpes suzette. Real vanilla ice cream is the ideal partner, but thick cream is an excellent understudy as long as it is really cold; part of the magic of this dish is the contrast in temperatures – hot, sizzling, caramelising sauce and cold cream or ice cream. Let the cream or ice cream melt slightly into the butter before you start eating as it will be very, very hot!

baked bananas with cointreau and pecans

75 g/3 oz/scant $1/3$ cup butter

50 g/2 oz/$1/4$ cup caster (superfine) sugar

Juice of $1/2$ lemon

Grated zest and juice of 1 large orange

15 ml/1 tbsp orange liqueur such as Cointreau or Grand Marnier

2 large bananas

50 g/2 oz/$1/2$ cup chopped, toasted pecan nuts

TO SERVE:

Vanilla ice cream or double (heavy) cream

Melt the butter in a small heavy-based saucepan.

Stir in the sugar, lemon juice, orange zest and juice and the liqueur. Simmer over very low heat for about ten minutes until the mixture is thick and syrupy.

Preheat the oven to 200°C/400°F/gas 6/fan oven 180°C.

Peel the bananas, cut them in half lengthways and then across into four pieces. Place them in two individual gratin dishes, about 13 cm/5 in diameter. Pour the orange butter over, then bake for 10 minutes until the bananas are soft and the butter is bubbling.

Sprinkle with the pecans and serve with vanilla ice cream or cream.

the foxtrot

The music and the pace are slowing down. The steps are becoming long, gliding and smooth, the appearance a trifle lazier and less hurried. The canter has become a trot, you feel vaguely under control and ready to enjoy yourself in the kitchen for an hour or so. Foxtrot *repas de deux* are for the kind of day when, for example:

◆ you did all the necessary shopping at the weekend
◆ the meeting was positive and finished promptly
◆ the visitors from Head Office were jet-lagged and decided to return to their hotel at five o'clock
◆ you are looking for an excuse not to clean the bathroom
◆ you arrive at the bus stop three minutes before the bus
◆ you remembered to take the fish out of the freezer the night before
◆ there is a parking space right outside the house
◆ the ironing basket is empty
◆ there is a wonderful play on the radio that you can listen to in the kitchen
◆ you have a pot of fresh, home-made, golden chicken stock in the refrigerator that you are just longing to make into a soup to remind you of the Ionian Sea

Dancing the foxtrot requires about an hour – sometimes slightly more, sometimes slightly less. The preparation takes a little longer: it may all have to be done in one go; or perhaps it can be divided into two stages if it is more convenient, as in soup or risotto or roasting an ingredient; or it may have to be staggered if, for instance, something needs to be marinated. But there is no need for real velocity and you can relax just a bit, or even quite a bit, and enjoy preparing your supper at a measured, steady rate.

Another classic Provençal sauce, aioli – meaning garlic and oil – is simply a garlicky mayonnaise. It is served as part of the Grand Aioli, a traditional meal of salt cod, vegetables and eggs.

The basic concept of mayonnaise flavoured with garlic can be expanded with the addition of other ingredients to give an aromatic and luscious sauce. Roasted chillies and red peppers give this particular aioli a spicy mellowness and a brick-red colour. It seems to have a strong affinity with barbecued food.

I like to make the mayonnaise base first with an electric whisk rather than in the food processor – it only takes a few minutes and, because the quantities are fairly small, it avoids the utter frustration of curdling and the resulting necessity to wash everything out and start all over again! I add an extra egg yolk for the same reason.

Try this aioli on a hamburger or salade niçoise, with chicken fajitas or tabbouleh mixed with Feta cheese, or stirred into a bowl of plain pasta.

provençal roasted red pepper aioli

1 large red (bell) pepper, about 200 g/7 oz

2 mild red chillies

1 garlic clove, peeled and crushed

2.5 ml/$\frac{1}{2}$ tsp Dijon mustard

1.5 ml/$\frac{1}{4}$ tsp balsamic vinegar

2 egg yolks

Sea salt and freshly ground black pepper

120 ml/4 fl oz/$\frac{1}{2}$ cup olive oil

Preheat the oven to 200°C/400°F/gas 6/fan oven 180°C.

Place the red pepper and chillies in a small baking dish and roast them for 10 minutes. Remove the chillies from the dish and set aside to cool.

Continue to cook the pepper for a further 30 minutes until soft and blackened in parts. Set it aside with the chillies.

While the peppers and chillies are cooking, make the basic aioli. Place the garlic, mustard, vinegar, egg yolks and some salt in a medium glass or china bowl. Whisk it all together with an electric beater, then start adding the oil a little at a time – I find the easiest way to do this is to put the oil in a jug and pour it from there. Continue whisking until all the oil is incorporated and you have a thick, glossy mayonnaise.

When the pepper and chillies are totally cooled, peel the pepper and remove the stalk and seeds. Halve the chillies and scrape out the seeds. Transfer the pepper and chillies to the bowl of a food processor and process until fairly smooth.

Add the mayonnaise to the pepper sauce in the food processor and whiz it all together. Taste for seasoning.

The aioli keeps well in a covered container in the fridge for 3 days before becoming decidedly bossy.

See also Sausages with Roasted Red Pepper Aioli (page 101) and Parma Ham, Tomato and Mozzarella Salad (page 67).

This lovely light soup is as much a part of Greek island holidays as Greek salad and souvlaki! I have added a Moroccan-inspired relish, which lifts it to new heights of freshness and sharpness.

It is important to use real stock here, rather than a cube or bouillon powder, as the simple, uncomplicated lemon flavour is easily overpowered.

avgolemono soup with pickled lemon relish

750 ml/1¼ pints/3 cups chicken stock

30 g/1 oz/2 tbsp brown basmati rice

1 egg

Juice of 1 lemon

Sea salt and freshly ground black pepper

FOR THE RELISH:

8 black olives, stoned (pitted) and quartered

2 pieces of Lemons Pickled in Salt and Lemon Juice (see page 19), finely chopped

10 g/scant ½ oz red onion, finely chopped

15 ml/1 tbsp olive oil

30 ml/2 tbsp finely chopped fresh parsley

Bring the stock to the boil in a medium saucepan, add the rice and simmer, covered, for 45 minutes.

Mix together the relish ingredients in a small bowl.

When the rice is cooked, whisk the egg and lemon juice with some seasoning in a heatproof bowl. Whisk in a ladleful of the hot stock, then a second one. Pour the egg mixture back into the stock, whisking all the time, and heat just until it thickens – do not let it boil or it will curdle.

Check the seasoning and serve in shallow bowls with a dollop of relish in the middle, adding the rest of the relish as you eat.

 This soup can also be served chilled.

Tzaziki is a traditional Greek hors d'oeuvre, delicious on its own with some warm pitta bread, or as an accompaniment to simple grilled (broiled) or oven-roasted Mediterranean vegetables.

It is available nowadays in tubs in supermarkets but it is quick and easy to make and a fresh, home-made tzaziki is light years away from the commercial stuff. In this recipe, it is dolloped into a bright green soup and, crunchy with cucumber and red onion, it is a perfect foil to the natural sweetness of the peas.

pea soup
with cucumber tzaziki

FOR THE SOUP:

30 ml/2 tbsp olive oil

200 g/7 oz white onions, peeled and roughly chopped

2 garlic cloves, peeled and roughly chopped

500 g/18 oz frozen peas

900 ml/1$\frac{1}{2}$ pints/3$\frac{3}{4}$ cups vegetable stock, or
    water with 5 ml/1 tsp bouillon powder

Sea salt and freshly ground black pepper

15 g/$\frac{1}{2}$ oz fresh mint

FOR THE TZAZIKI:

75 g/3 oz cucumber

1 garlic clove, peeled and crushed

25 g/1 oz red onion, finely chopped

15 g/$\frac{1}{2}$ oz fresh mint, coarsely chopped

30 ml/2 tbsp olive oil

250 ml/8 fl oz/1 cup Greek-style plain yoghurt

Sea salt and freshly ground black pepper

To make the soup, heat the oil in a saucepan. Add the onion and garlic and sweat them gently for about 10 minutes until softened – do not allow them to brown. Add the peas and stock, bring to the boil and simmer uncovered for 10 minutes. Season and set aside to cool.

While the soup is cooling, make the tzaziki. Halve and then quarter the cucumber lengthways, slice off and discard the seedy centre and dice the remaining flesh. Place it in a small bowl with the garlic, onion, mint, oil and yoghurt and mix well. (Season the tzaziki just before serving so that the cucumber does not go watery.)

Strip the mint leaves from the stalks and put them in the bowl of a food processor. Add the pea mixture and process until smooth.

Sieve (strain) the soup through the medium disc of a mouli-légumes. Now either chill the soup or reheat it gently.

Check the seasoning, ladle into bowls and serve with a good dollop of tzaziki, adding more as you eat.

 You can omit sieving the soup but it is well worth the little time it takes as one of the pleasures of this dish is the velvety smoothness of the soup with the crunchiness of the tzaziki.

This soup is just as good served chilled.

apple mulligatawny with coconut and cashew

50 g/2 oz/$\frac{1}{4}$ cup brown basmati rice

15 ml/1 tbsp olive oil

175 g/6 oz onions, peeled and roughly chopped

1 heaped tsp medium-hot curry paste

125 g/4$\frac{1}{2}$ oz tomatoes, skinned and quartered

175 g/6 oz eating (dessert) apples, peeled, cored and roughly chopped

Sea salt and freshly ground black pepper

1 x 400 g/14 oz/large can of coconut milk

120 ml/4 fl oz/$\frac{1}{2}$ cup water

25 g/1 oz/$\frac{1}{4}$ cup roasted cashew nuts, coarsely chopped

A handful of fresh coriander (cilantro) leaves

Cook the rice in salted boiling water for about 45 minutes until tender. Drain.

While the rice is cooking, heat the oil in a saucepan, add the onion and cook gently for about 15 minutes until the onion is softened and lightly browned.

Stir in the curry paste, cook for a further 2 minutes, then add the tomatoes and apples. Season to taste, cover and stew for 20 minutes, stirring occasionally.

Add the coconut milk to the saucepan, bring to the boil and simmer for 30 minutes. Allow to cool slightly, then transfer to a food processor and process until smooth.

Return the mixture to the saucepan, add the rice and water and check the seasoning. Bring back to the boil, then serve topped with the nuts and coriander leaves.

A lovely summer lunch with some good bread and a glass of chilled white wine! And, of course, if you already have some of the aioli in the fridge, you can turn this Foxtrot into a Quickstep. Other air-dried hams such as Serrano, San Daniele or Black Forest can be substituted if you prefer – they all have that smoky sweetness and spiciness which goes so well with the salad and aioli.

parma ham, tomato and mozzarella salad

250 g/9 oz plum cherry tomatoes, halved

2 spring onions (scallions), trimmed and thinly sliced

1 x 125 g/4^{1}/$_{2}$ oz Mozzarella cheese, drained and cut into 1 cm/^{1}/$_{2}$ in cubes

12 black olives, stoned (pitted) and halved

30 ml/2 tbsp olive oil

15 ml/1 tbsp chopped fresh parsley or snipped fresh chives

Sea salt and freshly ground black pepper

6 slices of Parma ham

1 quantity of Provençal Roasted Red Pepper Aioli (see page 64)

Gently mix together the tomatoes, onions, Mozzarella, olives, oil and herbs in a bowl. Season to taste and divide between two plates. Arrange the ham beside the salad and serve with the aioli.

The Swedes use soured (dairy sour) cream in their apple sauce, but I prefer the texture and mellow flavour of thick yoghurt.

This is a sharp and sweet salad, peppery with watercress and crunchy with golden almonds, which works really well with smoked salmon, cutting through its richness and enhancing its whiff of spice. And if you have any sauce left over, try it with muesli or porridge for breakfast – untraditional but incredibly good.

smoked salmon with apple and orange salad

FOR THE SAUCE:

325 g/11½ oz cooking (tart) apples, peeled, cored and cut into chunks

60 ml/4 tbsp water

100 ml/3½ fl oz/scant ½ cup Greek-style plain yoghurt

Runny honey, to taste

FOR THE SALAD:

15 g/½ oz/2 tbsp cup whole blanched almonds

1 large orange

1 small eating (dessert) apple

1 bunch of watercress

15 ml/1 tbsp olive oil

125 g/4½ oz smoked salmon

Heat the oven to 160°C/325°F/gas 3/fan oven 145°C.

Place the almonds in a small ovenproof dish and cook for about 15 minutes until golden brown. Leave to cool.

To make the sauce, place the cooking apples and water in a small saucepan and cook over a low heat, stirring occasionally, for about 20 minutes until thick. Allow to cool, then mix in the yoghurt and honey to taste.

Peel the orange, cut out the segments and place them in a small salad bowl, along with any juice. Quarter and core the eating apple, slice fairly thinly and add to the bowl.

Cut the watercress leaves from the stalks and fold the leaves into the fruit along with the oil and the almonds.

Arrange the salad and smoked salmon on two plates and serve with the sauce suédoise.

 You could make the sauce in advance; it will keep well in the fridge for a couple of days.

This earthy, colourful salad is pungent with the aromas and flavours of the Mediterranean.

Chick peas are one of the few pulses I do not cook from scratch because, however long I cook them, they never seem to soften sufficiently and have a chalky texture – so I just open a tin.

chick pea, roasted pepper and egg salad with tahini

1 red (bell) pepper, about 175 g/6 oz, seeded and cut into 1 cm/¹/₂ in wide strips

60 ml/4 tbsp olive oil

Sea salt and freshly ground black pepper

15 ml/1 tbsp dark tahini

150 ml/¹/₄ pint/²/₃ cup Greek-style plain yoghurt

1 x 400 g/14 oz/large can of chick peas (garbanzos), drained and rinsed

100 g/4 oz cherry tomatoes, halved

35 g/1¹/₂ oz red onion, peeled and finely chopped

1 garlic clove, peeled and crushed

15 ml/1 tbsp capers, rinsed, squeezed dry and roughly chopped

20 g/³/₄ oz black olives, stoned (pitted) and halved

30 ml/2 tbsp chopped fresh parsley

30 ml/2 tbsp chopped fresh coriander (cilantro)

2 hard-boiled (hard-cooked) eggs, peeled and quartered

Start by roasting the red pepper as this can be done well ahead of time. Preheat the oven to 180°C/350°F/gas 4/fan oven 160°C. Place the pepper strips in a small ovenproof dish, drizzle with 15 ml/1 tbsp of the oil, sprinkle with salt and pepper and bake for about 40 minutes until soft and slightly blackened at the edges. Allow to cool and set aside until needed.

Whisk the tahini into the yoghurt and add salt to taste. Set aside.

Place the roasted pepper strips, chick peas, tomatoes, onion, garlic, capers, olives, the remaining oil and the herbs in a roomy bowl. Season well and mix gently.

Pile the salad on to a large flat serving dish, garnish with the egg quarters and serve with the tahini yoghurt.

 In winter, you could serve this as a warm salad: bring a small saucepan of water to the boil, add the chick peas and bring back to the boil. Drain and toss with the other ingredients.

It always amazes me what a huge difference roasting the potatoes makes to the flavour and texture of the final dish. Having discovered this, I never make a potato salad nowadays with boiled or steamed potatoes.

This salad makes wonderful picnic food, savoury and sustaining, perfect for a long country walk or a lazy day at the beach; the pancetta may have lost some of its crispness by the time you get around to eating, but it will beat sandwiches or bread and cheese hands down!

roasted pepper, pancetta and new potato salad

400 g/14 oz large new potatoes, washed

1 red (bell) pepper, about 175 g/6 oz, seeded and cut into 1 cm/½ in wide strips

1 bay leaf

A sprig of rosemary

30 ml/2 tbsp olive oil

Sea salt and freshly ground black pepper

35 g/1½ oz sliced pancetta or streaky bacon rashers (slices), rinded

FOR THE PESTO:

15 g/½ oz fresh basil

1 garlic clove, peeled

25 g/1 oz/¼ cup freshly grated Parmesan cheese

150 ml/¼ pint/⅔ cup olive oil

25 g/1 oz/¼ cup pine nuts

Parmesan cheese shavings, to garnish

Preheat the oven to 220°C/425°F/gas 7/fan oven 200°C. Cut the potatoes into wedges and cook in salted boiling water for five minutes. Drain.

Place the pepper strips and potatoes in an ovenproof dish, tuck the herbs in among them, drizzle with the oil and season well. Roast in the oven for about 45 minutes, stirring occasionally, until the pepper is brown around the edges and the potatoes are crusty. Transfer to a salad bowl and set aside to cool.

Grill (broil) the pancetta or bacon until crisp and drain on kitchen paper (paper towels).

To make the pesto, place all the ingredients except the pine nuts in a food processor and process until smooth. Add the pine nuts and whizz for 5 seconds – you want to keep a bit of crunch. Taste for seasoning (you may not need any because Parmesan cheese is salty).

When you are ready to eat, mix the pesto into the potatoes and peppers, crumble the pancetta over and top with Parmesan cheese shavings.

Baked omelette is probably a better description than frittata, since I make this in the oven. A proper frittata, made in a frying pan on the hob, requires attention, careful heat control and a lot of manoeuvring when it comes to turning it out, because half the time the frittata will have stuck somewhere along the bottom! Pouring the egg mix into a well-buttered ramekin (custard cup) and baking it makes life infinitely less stressful.

caramelised onion, tomato and olive frittata

30 ml/2 tbsp olive oil, plus extra for drizzling

450 g/1 lb onions, peeled and thinly sliced

Sea salt and freshly ground black pepper

200 g/7 oz baby plum tomatoes, halved

6 eggs

16 black olives, stoned (pitted) and halved

50 g/2 oz Feta cheese

Butter for greasing

15 ml/1 tbsp snipped fresh chives

1 quantity of Green Olive and Oregano Tapenade (see page 18)

Heat the oil in a frying pan. Add the onions and plenty of seasoning and cook over a gentle heat, stirring occasionally, for about 30 minutes until soft and brown. Allow to cool slightly.

While the onions are cooking, preheat the oven to 200°C/400°F/gas 6/fan oven 180°C. Line a baking (cookie) sheet with baking parchment and arrange the tomatoes on it, cut-sides up. Sprinkle with salt and pepper, drizzle with oil and roast for 20 minutes until they are slightly wizened and starting to brown around the edges.

Leave the oven on while you assemble the frittata. Break the eggs into a bowl, add some seasoning and whisk well. Carefully stir in the onions, olives and tomatoes.

Pour the mixture into two well-greased 250 ml/8 fl oz/1 cup ramekins (custard cups). Crumble the cheese over the top, then bake for 20 minutes until firm to the touch.

Sprinkle with the chives and serve immediately with the tapenade.

 The onions, tomatoes and tapenade can be prepared up to 24 hours in advance.

If you fancy this as picnic food, it is very amenable to being transported in a rucksack – just wrap the ramekins well in clingfilm (plastic wrap).

The ideal way to cook the vegetables for the Catalán *escalivada* is on a barbecue as traditionally they are cooked in hot ashes. However, I find that a ridged cast-iron grill pan works very well, and it requires less cleaning! Failing that, you can simply cook them under a hot grill, but this is rather time-consuming.

Bearing in mind the above-mentioned hot ashes, several versions of *escalivada* that we were served in Barcelona were disappointing as the vegetables seemed to have been steamed or boiled rather than grilled in any way – they were pale, soft, mushy and rather tasteless. But our favourite tapas bar, Origens 99.9% in the La Ribera district of the old town, produced a perfect *escalivada*, piled on to a thick slice of toasted garlicky country bread and topped with big, fat Catalán anchovies. And the ideal accompaniment? A large glass of cold, sparkling *cava*!

catalán tosta de escalivada

1 large aubergine (eggplant), about 400 g/14 oz

300 g/11 oz onions

1 large red (bell) pepper, about 200 g/7 oz

1 large yellow pepper, about 200 g/7 oz

100 ml/3½ fl oz/scant ½ cup olive oil

4 thick slices of good heavy bread

1 large garlic clove, peeled

Sea salt and freshly ground black pepper

8 anchovy fillets

Top and tail the aubergine and cut it lengthways into slices about 7.5 mm/ ⅓ in thick, discarding the end ones as they will be more skin than flesh.

Top and tail the onions and cut them across into slices about 1 cm/½ in thick. Remove the skins.

Halve the peppers and remove the stem and seeds, then cut them into slices about 2 cm/¾ in wide.

Preheat the oven to its lowest setting and put in a roasting tray to warm.

Brush all the vegetables with some of the oil. Heat a ridged cast-iron grill pan and cook the vegetables for 2–3 minutes on each side until they are nicely coloured. A pair of tongs is ideal for flipping them over, particularly the onions, which tend to fall apart if you use a spatula. Turning the vegetables at an 180° angle once will give you a nice criss-crossed pattern. As you finish cooking each batch, transfer it to the tray in the oven to keep warm.

When the vegetables are all cooked, toast the bread on both sides and rub one side well with the clove of garlic.

Drizzle the remaining oil over the bread, then pile on the vegetables, seasoning as you go. Arrange the anchovy fillets on top and serve immediately.

The faint sweetness of the blinis works really well with the salty, smoky accompaniments. Although the blinis can be made ahead of time and reheated, they are quick to make and infinitely nicer when fresh – and our favourite time to eat them is Sunday brunch.

Although I have used the Russian name 'blini' in this recipe, the idea came from a sweetcorn 'hotcake' that we once ate for breakfast in the beautiful Mexican colonial town of Oaxaca. On this occasion, they were served with soured cream, bacon and a palate-tingling chilli salsa.

sweetcorn blinis with smoked salmon and greek salata

15 ml/1 tbsp olive oil, plus extra for greasing

175 g/6 oz red onions, peeled and coarsely chopped

200 g/7 oz canned or frozen sweetcorn

2 eggs, beaten

250 ml/8 fl oz/1 cup milk

100 g/4 oz instant polenta (cornmeal)

75 g/3 oz/³/₄ cup wholemeal flour

7.5 ml/1¹/₂ tsp sea salt

Freshly ground black pepper

200 g/7 oz smoked salmon

1 quantity of Greek Salata with Fresh Herbs (see page 20)

Heat the oil in a small saucepan, add the onions and fry over a medium heat for 10 minutes, stirring occasionally, until soft but not brown. Allow to cool slightly, then place in a bowl with the sweetcorn, eggs, milk, polenta, flour, salt and a grinding of pepper. Mix well.

Preheat the oven to its lowest setting. Brush a crêpe pan with oil and heat it over a medium heat until the oil starts to shimmer. Ladle in a quarter of the blini batter and cook for about 1 minute until the underside is golden. Flip the blini over with a spatula and cook the other side for 1 minute. Keep warm in the oven while you make three more blinis.

To serve, place two blinis on each plate. Top with smoked salmon and the salata and eat promptly.

 A small heavy-based crêpe pan, about 10 cm/4 in across, is ideal as you can measure in the exact amount of batter but, failing that, use a small non-stick frying pan or omelette pan and pour in the batter in two stages: start off with an eighth of the batter, wait for about 30 seconds for the bottom to set and then carefully pour another eighth on top of the first – this way you will get a nice thick blini rather than a pancake.

Quesadillas are a tortilla turnover, served at every street stall, market *fonda* and restaurant in Mexico. The filling always includes cheese – *queso* is Spanish for cheese – but other than that the possibilities are endless. They are crisp and crunchy, rich and savoury, and straightforward to prepare, despite the length of the recipe.

Chipotle sauce is available from delicatessens and the speciality section of large supermarkets.

pancetta and goats' cheese quesadillas

makes four quesadillas

FOR THE SALSA:

400 g/14 oz tomatoes

3 garlic cloves, peeled

30 ml/2 tbsp olive oil

5 ml/1 tsp chipotle chilli sauce

Sea salt and freshly ground black pepper

FOR THE QUESADILLAS:

45 ml/3 tbsp olive oil

100 g/4 oz chopped pancetta or smoked bacon

150 g/5 oz red onions, peeled and sliced

1 red (bell) pepper, about 175 g/6 oz, seeded and cut into 1 cm/$\frac{1}{2}$ in wide strips

Sea salt and freshly ground black pepper

200 g/7 oz fresh goats' cheese

100 g/4 oz/1 cup freshly grated mature Cheddar (Monterey Jack) cheese

4 large corn tortillas

60 ml/4 tbsp chopped fresh coriander (cilantro)

To make the salsa, heat the grill (broiler) to high. Halve the tomatoes, put them cut-sides up in a baking dish and tuck the garlic cloves in among them. Grill (broil) about 10 cm/4 in from the heat for 15 minutes or until the tomatoes are soft and blackened along the edges.

Transfer to the bowl of a food processor, along with any juices, and process until fairly smooth.

Heat the oil in a saucepan, add the tomatoes, chipotle and some seasoning and cook, stirring occasionally, for about 10 minutes until the salsa thickens and darkens.

To make the quesadillas, heat a frying pan, add the oil and brown the pancetta or bacon in it for about 5 minutes.

Add the onions and pepper strips and cook, stirring occasionally, until the onion is translucent and the pepper soft. Season to taste.

Mix the two cheeses together.

When you are ready to cook the quesadillas, heat a large frying pan and place one tortilla in it. Spread a quarter of the cheese mixture over half the tortilla, top it with a quarter of the vegetable mixture and fold the second half of the tortilla over the filling to make a semi-circle. Repeat with a second tortilla.

Press gently down on each quesadilla with a spatula and cook them for 3 minutes. Flip them over carefully and brown the other side. Remove to a plate and keep warm in the oven while you make the other two.

Sprinkle the quesadillas with the coriander and serve with the salsa.

 Both the salsa and the vegetables and bacon can be prepared a couple of days ahead, chilled and reheated just before serving.

This Tunisian grilled vegetable salad, contrary to its name, is not a salad as such. The best description, although it does not make it sound particularly enticing, is a spicy mess of mashed grilled vegetables! Garnished with hard-boiled eggs, capers, olives, red onion and tuna flakes, Tunisians serve it cold as a first course and it is absolutely delicious.

At its simplest, it consists of just peppers and tomatoes, but virtually every town in Tunisia has its own version and we tasted many variations when we were there on holiday a few years ago. Green peppers are normally used, giving the salad a rather attractive bitterness. However, red peppers are just as good and produce a better colour and a richer, rounder flavour. Don't be put off by the long list of ingredients – it is easy to prepare, although the vegetables do take time to cook, as I prefer to roast some of them, because it is easier than grilling.

tunisian
salade méchouia

1 red (bell) pepper, about 175 g/6 oz

1 yellow pepper, about 175 g/6 oz

1 small aubergine (eggplant), about 275 g/10 oz, cut into 1 cm/½ in chunks

300 g/11 oz courgettes (zucchini), sliced into 1 cm/½ in thick discs

75 ml/5 tbsp olive oil, plus extra for drizzling

Sea salt and freshly ground black pepper

250 g/9 oz tomatoes, quartered

5 ml/1 tsp runny honey

5 ml/1 tsp cumin seeds

2.5 ml/½ tsp sweet paprika

100 g/4 oz canned tuna

15 g/½ oz red onion, thinly sliced

30 ml/2 tbsp chopped fresh parsley

15 ml/1 tbsp capers, rinsed and squeezed dry

10 black olives, stoned (pitted) and halved

2 hard-boiled (hard-cooked) eggs, peeled and quartered

TO SERVE:

Bread

Heat the grill (broiler) to high. Place the peppers on a baking (cookie) sheet and grill (broil) them 10 cm/4 in from the heat until they are blackened and blistered on all sides. Allow to cool, then remove the skin, stem and seeds. Set aside until all the vegetables are done.

Preheat the oven to 200°C/400°F/gas 6/fan oven 180°C. Place the aubergine and courgettes in a roasting tray, drizzle with 45 ml/3 tbsp of the oil and season well.

Place the tomatoes on a baking sheet lined with baking parchment and drizzle them first with 5 ml/1 tsp of the oil and then the honey. Season well.

Place both lots of vegetables in the oven. Roast for about 1 hour until the aubergine and courgettes are soft and golden and the tomatoes are soft and starting to blacken along the edges. Stir the aubergine and courgettes occasionally during cooking.

While the vegetables are cooking, toast the cumin seeds in a small, dry pan until aromatic – this will really bring out their flavour. Tip them into a mortar, add the paprika, and grind them fairly coarsely – they need to retain some texture.

When the vegetables are all cooked, place them together in a shallow dish, add the remaining oil and mash it all up with a large fork or a potato masher – or, even easier in my opinion, use an ordinary knife and fork to cut it up, rather like cutting up food for a small child. Check the seasoning.

Sprinkle with the cumin and paprika, then the tuna, onion and parsley, and finally the capers and olives. Garnish with the egg and serve warm or at room temperature with plenty of bread to scoop it up.

Salade Méchouia is also excellent as part of a Tunisian mezze plate, with perhaps a square of Tunisian Tagine Méchouia (see page 109) and some grilled Merguez sausages.

Big, dark portabello mushrooms have a lovely meaty texture, and roasting them in olive oil really brings out their woodsy flavour. This is the kind of dish that can be assembled a couple of hours ahead of time and left to sit patiently while you sort out the rest of your life – then it can just be popped into the oven when it suits you.

cheesy baked portabello mushrooms with herb pesto

4 large portabello mushrooms

60 ml/4 tbsp olive oil

2 garlic cloves, peeled and thinly sliced

Sea salt and freshly ground black pepper

300 g/11 oz tomatoes

100 g/4 oz fresh goats' cheese

1 x 125 g/4$\frac{1}{2}$ oz Mozzarella cheese, thinly sliced

50 g/2 oz/1 cup fresh wholemeal breadcrumbs

40 g/1$\frac{3}{4}$ oz freshly grated Parmesan cheese

20 g/$\frac{3}{4}$ oz/3 tbsp pine nuts

FOR THE PESTO:

15 g/$\frac{1}{2}$ oz fresh basil

15 g/$\frac{1}{2}$ oz fresh flatleaf parsley

1 garlic clove, peeled

30 g/1 oz/$\frac{1}{4}$ cup freshly grated Parmesan cheese

150 ml/$\frac{1}{4}$ pint/$\frac{2}{3}$ cup olive oil

Sea salt and freshly ground black pepper

20 g/$\frac{3}{4}$ oz/3 tbsp pine nuts

Preheat the oven to 200°C/400°F/gas 6/fan oven 180°C. Peel the mushrooms and place them white-side down in a baking dish. Drizzle with half the oil and sprinkle with the garlic and some salt and pepper. Bake for 15 minutes.

Cut the tomatoes into slices about ½ cm/¼ in thick and arrange them on top of the mushrooms. Season them well, crumble the goats' cheese over and top with the Mozzarella slices.

Mix the breadcrumbs with the Parmesan, the remaining oil and the pine nuts and pat the mixture on top of the mushrooms (don't worry if some of the mix ends up in the bottom of the baking dish – it will soak up the delicious juices from the mushrooms). Bake on the top shelf for about 20 minutes until the breadcrumbs are browned and crisp.

Meanwhile, to make the pesto, place all the ingredients except the pine nuts in the bowl of a food processor and process until fairly smooth. Check the seasoning, then add the pine nuts and process for just a few seconds so that they keep some of their texture and give the pesto a bit of crunch.

Serve the mushrooms with a good spoonful of the pesto on top.

Mussels and cream are made for each other, and the chorizo and tomatoes in this recipe add two more layers of flavour, savoury and sharp, to enhance the sweetness of the mussels and the richness of the cream.

The best way to eat mussels is to use an empty shell as a pincer to pull the mussels from their shell – but it's a messy business so have plenty of napkins available!

mussels with saffron and chorizo

1 kg/2¼ lb shell-on mussels

150 g/5 oz cherry tomatoes, halved

125 g/4½ oz chorizo, diced

15 ml/1 tbsp olive oil

250 g/9 oz onions, peeled and coarsely chopped

250 ml/8 fl oz/1 cup white wine

250 ml/8 fl oz/1 cup double (heavy) cream

Sea salt and freshly ground black pepper

2.5 ml/½ tsp saffron strands

30 ml/2 tbsp chopped fresh parsley

Scrub the mussels and remove the beards. Discard any that are broken.

Preheat the oven to 200°C/400°F/gas 6/fan oven 180°C. Place the tomato halves cut-sides up in a roasting tray lined with baking parchment and roast them for 45 minutes until slightly shrivelled and starting to blacken around the edges (this concentrates their flavour and sweetness).

Fry the chorizo in a heavy-based frying pan over a medium heat for about 10 minutes, stirring occasionally, until golden. Using a slotted spoon, remove it to a plate lined with kitchen paper to drain; discard the fat.

Heat the oil in a saucepan large enough to hold the mussels later on, stir in the onions and cook gently for about 10 minutes until soft but not brown.

Turn up the heat, pour in the wine and let it bubble fiercely for a few minutes. Add the cream and some seasoning, bring it back to the boil, then turn the heat down to low again and simmer for about 20 minutes until really thick – stir it often towards the end as it will start to stick.

Add the chorizo, saffron and tomatoes, then put the mussels in on top. Cover with a lid, turn up the heat to high again, and cook undisturbed for 3 minutes, by which time the mussels should have opened and released lots of delicious juice to mingle with the rich, savoury cream.

Remove from the heat, sprinkle with the parsley and, using a large spoon, turn the mussels over and over in the sauce to coat them well.

Serve immediately in large, shallow soup bowls. You will need spoons to finish off the sauce.

prawns in wine and garlic cream

Utter indulgence! Rich, mellow, fabulously satisfying. The simplicity of the flavours in this dish is its greatest charm. The idea came from a wonderful garlic soup we ate in Barcelona – it was bold and aromatic, and garnished with just one giant grilled (broiled) *gamba*, as the huge Spanish prawns are called.

20 large garlic cloves, peeled

150 ml/¹/₄ pint/²/₃ cup white wine

250 ml/8 fl oz/1 cup double (heavy) cream

200 g/7 oz raw king prawns (shrimp), shelled and deveined

Sea salt and freshly ground black pepper

15 ml/1 tbsp chopped fresh parsley

Preheat the oven to 200°C/400°F/gas 6/fan oven 180°C.

Place the garlic in a small ovenproof dish, cover tightly with foil and bake for 45 minutes, by which time it will be soft and luscious. Mash thoroughly with a fork.

While the garlic is cooking, place the wine in a small, non-corrosive saucepan and reduce it over medium heat to a couple of tablespoonfuls. Add the cream and reduce by half. Stir in the garlic, then the prawns and cook gently just until the prawns turn pink and firm.

Season, sprinkle with the parsley and serve immediately.

A risotto needs attention and there is no point in embarking on one unless you can give it the necessary time – if you are in the least bit doubtful about having the leisure to treat it with TLC, keep it for a Waltzing day! It's not that it's particularly complicated to make or that there is a lot of cooking involved but, while it is cooking, you need to stand over it most of the time and stir it frequently. Whenever I make risotto in a hurry, I always end up by ruining it: chalky grains or mushy grains or sloppy grains!

So make this dish when you have at least one calm, uncluttered hour ahead of you and then sit down to enjoy the perfection of a tender and creamy risotto – without delay because risotto does not like to be kept waiting and goes unpleasantly solid and lumpy very quickly once it is taken off the heat. The whole process of adding liquid to a risotto and waiting for it to be absorbed takes about 30 minutes.

Always use asparagus in season for best results. This risotto also works very well with frozen peas instead of asparagus.

asparagus, king prawn and smoked salmon risotto

75 g/3 oz asparagus tips

40 g/1³/₄ oz butter

1 shallot, about 20 g/³/₄ oz, peeled and finely chopped

1 garlic clove, peeled and sliced

175 g/6 oz/³/₄ cup risotto rice

100 ml/3¹/₂ fl oz/scant ¹/₂ cup white wine

400 ml/14 fl oz/1³/₄ cups fish or chicken stock, heated

40 g/1³/₄ oz freshly grated Parmesan cheese

100 g/4 oz raw king prawns (shrimp), shelled and deveined

75 g/3 oz smoked salmon, cut into strips

Sea salt and freshly ground black pepper

15 ml/1 tbsp chopped fresh parsley

Parmesan cheese shavings, to garnish

Bring a pan of salted water to a good rolling boil and add the asparagus. Cook for 2 minutes, drain and refresh under cold running water. Set aside.

Melt 15 g/¹/₂ oz of the butter in a large heavy-based pan, add the shallot and garlic and cook gently until softened but not browned.

Stir in the rice and cook for 10 minutes, stirring to coat it well in the butter.

Add the wine and cook, stirring occasionally, until the rice has absorbed the wine. Add a good ladleful of the stock and, again, cook and stir until it has been absorbed. Continue in this way until the stock is all used up and the rice is creamy and tender but still firm.

Add the grated Parmesan cheese, asparagus, prawns and smoked salmon and cook for a few minutes longer until the prawns just turn pink.

Taste for seasoning, stir in the remaining butter and serve immediately, sprinkled with the parsley and garnished with the Parmesan shavings.

roast seabass with creamy leek and saffron risotto

500 g/18 oz leeks

50 g/2 oz/¼ cup butter

1 x 500 g/18 oz seabass, scaled and gutted

5 ml/1 tsp olive oil

Sea salt and freshly ground black pepper

600 ml/1 pint/2½ cups hot fish, chicken or vegetable stock, or hot water with 15 ml/1 tbsp bouillon powder

2.5 ml/½ tsp saffron strands

200 g/7 oz risotto rice

120 ml/4 fl oz/½ cup white wine

50 g/2 oz/½ cup freshly grated Parmesan cheese

30 ml/2 tbsp Mascarpone cheese

Trim the leeks, discarding any roots and the dark green part – you should end up with about 350 g/12 oz. Split them in half almost down to the root end and wash well to get rid of any grit. Shake to remove any excess water and cut into 1 cm/½ in slices.

Melt the butter in a medium saucepan, add the leeks and cook fairly briskly, stirring occasionally, for about 10 minutes until softened but not browned.

While the leeks are cooking, rinse the seabass under cold running water, washing any trace of blood out of the cavity. Pat dry with kitchen paper (paper towels) and place on a foil-lined baking (cookie) sheet. Rub the oil over the skin and season well. Set aside. Preheat the oven to 200°C/400°F/gas 6/fan oven 180°C.

Have your stock ready and heated to simmering point and stir in the saffron.

Add the rice to the leeks, stirring well to coat the grains with butter. Pour in the wine and cook, stirring occasionally, until the rice has absorbed the wine.

Add a good ladleful of the stock and, again, cook and stir until the liquid has been absorbed. Continue in this way until the stock is all used up and the rice is creamy and tender but still firm.

Seabass is somehow an ideal partner for risotto because of its delicate, soft flesh; mackerel is also good and considerably cheaper. You can also, of course, use fillets, which makes it all easier at serving time and improves the presentation no end, but fish cooked whole and on the bone seems to retain infinitely more flavour – and flavour features much higher on my priority list than appearance.

See my notes on Asparagus, King Prawn and Smoked Salmon Risotto (page 87) for making sure you give a risotto the time and attention it deserves.

Ten minutes into the risotto, place the seabass in the oven and roast for 15 minutes.

Season the risotto and stir in the two cheeses. Remove from the heat, cover and allow to rest for a couple of minutes.

Test the seabass with your thumb – it should be soft to the touch. Remove the top fillet by running a sharp knife along the backbone and then lifting it with a spatula on to a warm plate. Pull out the backbone and place the bottom fillet on a second plate. Do not worry if the fillets break up a bit and look messy, it really doesn't matter!

Serve immediately with the risotto.

If you are not a garlic lover, turn the page as this recipe is definitely not for you! Skordalia is a Greek sauce, saturated in garlic and thickened with either bread or potato. I find the texture of the potato version more appealing.

If you close your eyes, the aromas and flavours of this dish will transport you instantly to a harbour-side taverna!

grilled swordfish with greek salata and skordalia

175 g/6 oz potatoes, peeled and cut into 2 cm/³/₄ in chunks

2 garlic cloves, peeled and crushed

Sea salt and freshly ground black pepper

120 ml/4 fl oz/¹/₂ cup olive oil, plus extra for brushing

Fresh lemon juice or white wine vinegar

2 swordfish steaks, about 200 g/7 oz each and about 2 cm/³/₄ in thick

1 quantity of Greek Salata with Fresh Herbs (see page 20)

Start off with the skordalia as the potatoes need to be cold. Steam the potatoes until soft and allow to cool completely.

Place the potatoes in a bowl and mash them with a potato masher or a wooden spoon. Add the garlic and some seasoning and then, with an electric whisk, slowly whisk in the oil.

Add a good squeeze of lemon juice or about 2.5 ml/¹/₂ tsp vinegar and taste, adding more if necessary to give the sauce a bit of bite. If the skordalia is rather thick – and it will be if the potatoes were very floury – add a spoonful or two of water until it is just a tiny bit sloppy but not runny.

Heat a ridged cast-iron grill pan until really hot. Brush the swordfish with oil, season and place in the pan, pressing down with a spatula. Cook for 1 minute, then swivel the steaks around 180° and press down again (this will create a nice criss-cross pattern) and cook for a further 2 minutes. Flip the steaks over and cook the other side in the same way.

Serve with the skordalia and Greek Salata.

 You can use 200 g/7 oz of leftover cold mashed potato or even peeled boiled potatoes if you want.

When I first started putting this recipe together, I wondered whether the gutsy salsa would overpower the fish, but it works remarkably well, and the colours are so pretty!

Salsa Puttanesca, named after the red light district, is usually a cooked tomato sauce for pasta, but I have reworked it along the lines of a Mexican salsa with Italian ingredients. You can use salmon rather than red snapper, if you prefer.

red snapper with puy lentils and salsa puttanesca

200 g/7 oz Puy lentils

2 thick lemon slices

45 ml/1½ tbsp olive oil

2 red snapper fillets, skin on, about 200 g/7 oz each and 2 cm/¾ in thick

Sea salt and freshly ground black pepper

15 ml/1 tbsp olive oil

FOR THE SALSA:

125 g/4½ oz cherry tomatoes, halved

2 anchovy fillets, coarsely chopped (scissors make it easier)

1 garlic clove, peeled and crushed

15 ml/1 tbsp capers, rinsed, squeezed dry and coarsely chopped

10 black olives, stoned (pitted) and halved

30 ml/2 tbsp parsley, chopped

Preheat the oven to 200°C/400°F/gas 6/fan oven 180°C. Line a baking (cookie) sheet with baking parchment.

To make the salsa, place the cherry tomatoes, cut-sides up, on the sheet. Season well and bake for 30 minutes until soft and slightly blackened along the edges. Allow to cool, then place in a small bowl.

While the tomatoes are cooking, rinse the lentils under cold running water and place in a medium saucepan. Add the lemon slices, cover with water, bring to the boil and simmer for 30 minutes. Drain, return to the saucepan, season and mix in 30 ml/2 tbsp of the oil. Cover and set aside while you cook the fish – the lentils will keep warm for some time.

Heat the remaining oil in a non-stick frying pan over a highish heat. Season the fish and cook it, skin-side down, for about 3 minutes. Turn it over carefully with a spatula and cook the other side for a further 3 minutes. If your fillets are quite thin, adjust the cooking time – test them with your thumb; they should be firm with a very slight bounce.

Meanwhile, add the remaining salsa ingredients to the tomatoes and toss gently.

As soon as it is cooked, serve the red snapper on a bed of Puy lentils and top with the salsa.

An unoriginal but staunch favourite! There's something so relaxed and summery about this dish – good ingredients simply prepared.

Anchoïade is a Provençal, mayonnaise-based sauce, but I like to make it with yoghurt; it is quicker, sharper and lighter. Don't be tempted to use anchovy purée because you will lose the texture of the chopped anchovies and their sudden burst of flavour.

grilled salmon salade niçoise

250 g/9 oz new potatoes, scrubbed and halved if large

Sea salt and freshly ground black pepper

75 ml/5 tbsp olive oil, plus extra for brushing

20 g/³/₄ oz red onion, peeled and thinly sliced

1 garlic clove, peeled and crushed

175 g/6 oz cherry tomatoes, halved (a mixture of red and yellow is pretty)

10 black olives, stoned (pitted) and halved

15 ml/1 tbsp capers, rinsed and squeezed dry

250 g/9 oz thin French (green) beans, topped, tailed and cut in half

2 x 200 g/7 oz pieces of salmon fillet, about 2 cm/³/₄ in thick, skinned

15 g/¹/₂ oz fresh mint or basil, coarsely chopped

15 g/¹/₂ oz fresh flatleaf parsley, coarsely chopped

4 hard-boiled (hard-cooked) quails' eggs, peeled and halved
or 1 hard-boiled egg, peeled and quartered

FOR THE ANCHOÏADE:

150 ml/¹/₄ pint/²/₃ cup Greek-style plain yoghurt

1 garlic clove, peeled and crushed

5 anchovy fillets, finely chopped

30 ml/2 tbsp olive oil

Sea salt and freshly ground black pepper

Preheat the oven to 200°C/400°F/gas 6/fan oven 180°C. Cook the potatoes in salted boiling water for 5 minutes, drain well, and place in a roasting tin.

Season, drizzle with 30 ml/2 tbsp of the oil and toss well to ensure that they are evenly coated. Roast in the oven, stirring occasionally, for about 40 minutes until golden and slightly crusty.

Make the anchoïade while the potatoes are cooking by mixing together all the ingredients.

Place the onion, garlic, tomatoes, olives, capers and the remaining oil in a large bowl.

When the potatoes are almost ready, cook the beans in salted boiling water for 5 minutes, drain and rinse briefly under cold running water to refresh them. Add them to the large bowl.

Brush the salmon fillets with oil, season them lightly and place them on a foil-lined baking (cookie) sheet. Heat the grill (broiler) to high and grill (broil) the fillets 10 cm/4 in from the heat for about 7 minutes – test them for doneness by pressing them with your thumb; they should be firm with a bit of bounce still left in them.

Add the potatoes, herbs and some seasoning to the large bowl, and toss everything gently. Divide the salad between two warm plates, garnish with the eggs and place a salmon fillet on top. Drizzle the lot with anchoïade and serve immediately. Offer the rest of the anchoïade separately.

If you really don't like anchovies, serve the salmon with Provençal Roasted Red Pepper Aioli (see page 64).

Marinating the chicken with a bit of chilli, garlic and lime gives it the necessary oomph to stand up to the bold, lively purée and chutney. If you cannot find chipotle chilli sauce (usually available from delicatessens or the speciality section of large supermarkets), use any other chilli sauce, but the smokiness of the chipotle works particularly well here.

You may need a fair bit of lime juice in the sweet potatoes, as they can be quite cloying; their sweetness needs to be kept in the background – more of an undertone than obvious bravado! So buy at least two limes.

grilled chicken with sweet potato purée and coriander

15 ml/1 tbsp olive oil

1 garlic clove, peeled and crushed

15 ml/1 tbsp fresh lime juice

1 heaped tsp chipotle chilli sauce

2 chicken supremes

10 g/scant $^1/_2$ oz pine nuts

FOR THE PURÉE:

500 g/18 oz sweet potato, peeled and cut into 2 cm/$^3/_4$ in chunks

15 ml/1 tbsp olive oil

Sea salt and freshly ground black pepper

75 ml/5 tbsp Greek-style plain yoghurt

Fresh lime juice

FOR THE CHUTNEY:

100 ml/3$^1/_2$ fl oz/scant $^1/_2$ cup Greek-style plain yoghurt

40 g/1$^3/_4$ oz fresh coriander (cilantro), very coarsely chopped

1 hot red or green chilli, seeded

1 garlic clove, peeled

25 g/1 oz red onion, peeled and coarsely chopped

15 ml/1 tbsp olive oil

Preheat the oven to 200°C/400°F/gas 6/fan oven 180°C.

Mix together the oil, garlic, lime juice and chipotle sauce in a china or glass heat-resistant dish. Add the chicken and coat it well in the marinade. Set aside.

To make the purée, place the sweet potato in a roasting tin, drizzle with the oil and season well. Place in the oven and roast, stirring occasionally, for about 1 hour until soft and golden.

About 10 minutes before the end of the potato cooking time, place the pine nuts in a small roasting tin and put them on the floor of the oven. Cook them until golden. Allow to cool.

While the potatoes are cooking, make the chutney by placing all the ingredients in a food processor and processing until smooth and bright green. Add seasoning to taste and set aside.

When the sweet potatoes are ready, scrape them into a food processor, add the yoghurt and process until smooth. Check the seasoning and sharpen to taste with lime juice. Turn the oven off, transfer the purée to a small ovenproof dish and keep it warm in the oven until you are ready to serve.

When the purée and chutney are ready, preheat the grill (broiler) to high. Turn the chicken over once or twice in its marinade and cook it, still in its dish, about 10 cm/4 in from the heat for 5 minutes on each side until it is firm to the touch. Remove the dish from the grill (broiler), cover the chicken with a tea towel (dish cloth) and leave it to rest for 10 minutes before slicing into four or five thick slices.

Divide the purée between two warm plates. Place the sliced chicken on top of the purée and drizzle first with the cooking juices and then with some chutney. Scatter the pine nuts on top. Serve immediately with more chutney on the side.

If you have some leftover tapenade in the fridge, you can Quickstep through this recipe in no time at all.

Boursin, being a soft cheese, is not easy to slice so use it straight from the fridge or even give it a 15-minute blast in the freezer. Don't worry if it still crumbles and falls to pieces, just pat it over the tapenade as evenly as you can – the pancetta will cover up the mess!

chicken with olive tapenade, boursin and pancetta

2 chicken supremes

1 quantity of Green Olive and Oregano Tapenade (see page 18)

75 g/3 oz Boursin cheese with garlic and herbs

6 rashers (slices) of smoked pancetta

Preheat the oven to 200°C/400°F/gas 6/fan oven 180°C. Line a roasting tin with foil and lay the chicken supremes on it. Using the back of a teaspoon, carefully spread a good layer of tapenade all over the chicken.

Slice the Boursin as thinly as possible and arrange the slices on top of the tapenade. Top each supreme with three rashers of pancetta (two in an x-shape and the third one down the middle looks nice).

Bake the chicken in the oven for 15 minutes – the cheese will have melted to a rich, gooey softness and the pancetta will be crisp and savoury. Turn off the oven and leave the chicken to rest in there with the door ajar for 10 minutes.

Using a wide spatula, carefully transfer the chicken to two warm plates and serve immediately, with any leftover tapenade if you wish.

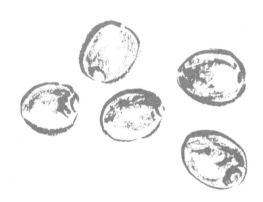

Brasserie chicken curry – an old-fashioned straightforward, soothing dish that we have eaten often in France, in typical neighbourhood-type restaurants full of locals and Gauloises' smoke. I call it old-fashioned because it is so unauthentic, flavoured with nothing more than curry powder or paste (forget about roasting and grinding several different, traditional spices!) and served with naff accompaniments such as peanuts, raisins and chopped bananas rather than raitas, chatnis and pickled relishes.

I use coconut milk and creamed coconut in my version for a greater roundness of flavour, but I have to admit that the French varieties I have eaten over the years have always been made with plenty of thick cream!

poulet à l'indienne with coconut milk

15 ml/1 tbsp vegetable oil

2 large chicken drumsticks and 2 large chicken thighs

300 g/11 oz onions, peeled and sliced

200 g/7 oz baby spinach leaves, washed

30 ml/2 tbsp Madras curry paste

Sea salt and freshly ground black pepper

5 ml/1 tsp bouillon powder

1 x 400 g/14 oz/large can of coconut milk

250 g/9 oz tomatoes, coarsely chopped

75 g/3 oz creamed coconut, coarsely chopped

TO SERVE:

Basmati rice, roasted salted peanuts, raisins, thick banana slices

Heat the oil in a frying pan over a medium heat and brown the chicken pieces well on all sides. Remove them with a slotted spoon to a plate. Add the onions to the pan and cook them over a gentle heat, stirring occasionally, for about 20 minutes until soft and golden.

While the onions are browning, cook the spinach in a large dry pan until it is wilted and dark green. Transfer it to a sieve (strainer) and push down on it with a large spoon to extract as much liquid as possible. Set aside.

Stir the curry paste into the onions and cook for a further 2 minutes. Return the chicken to the pan, add some seasoning and the bouillon powder, then pour in the coconut milk. Cover the pan, turn the heat right down, and leave it to simmer for 30 minutes.

Turn up the heat to medium and add the tomatoes and creamed coconut. Cook for a further 5 minutes, stirring, until the creamed coconut has melted and the tomatoes softened. Stir in the spinach and check the seasoning.

Serve immediately with rice, peanuts, raisins and banana.

duck with pomegranate and pistachio relish

15 ml/1 tbsp vegetable oil

2 duck breast fillets, about 200 g/7 oz each

10 ml/2 tsp runny honey

15 ml/1 tbsp sea salt flakes (not crystals)

FOR THE RELISH:

15 g/¹/₂ oz/2 tbsp shelled pistachio nuts

Sea salt

Olive oil

25 g/1 oz/2 tbsp caster (superfine) sugar

30 ml/2 tbsp water

15 ml/1 tbsp wine vinegar or cider vinegar

175 g/6 oz red onion, peeled and coarsely chopped

Seeds and juice from 1 pomegranate

Start off with the relish as it needs to cool down before you can add the pomegranate. Preheat the oven to 160°C/325°F/gas 3/fan oven 145°C. Place the pistachios in a small baking dish, sprinkle with a little salt and stir in 2.5 ml/¹/₂ tsp oil. Roast for 15 minutes. Set aside to cool, then chop coarsely.

While the pistachios are roasting, place the sugar in a small heavy-based saucepan with the water. Stir to dissolve the sugar and bring to the boil. Turn the heat right down and simmer until golden – watch it like a hawk as it burns easily and then you'll have to start all over again!

Remove the saucepan from the heat and add first the vinegar – stand well back as it will hiss and splutter (rubber gloves are a great help here) – and then the onion and pomegranate juice. Stir well and return to the heat. Continue to cook gently for about 10 minutes until the onion is soft and most of the liquid has evaporated. Allow to cool, then stir in a little salt, the pomegranate seeds and 15 ml/1 tbsp of olive oil.

Pomegranates, with their shiny leathery skins and scarlet jewelled interiors, are a blessing in winter when the selection of seasonal fruit is limited. They add colour, crunch and a sweet, aromatic freshness to fruit salads, puddings and sauces. One of my favourite breakfasts is thick tart yoghurt drizzled with Greek honey and the juice and seeds of a pomegranate.

Heat the vegetable oil in a frying pan and brown the flesh side of the duck breasts over a high heat for 2–3 minutes to seal.

Preheat the grill (broiler) to high. Transfer the duck to a foil-lined roasting tray, skin-side up, and spread the honey over the skin, then sprinkle with the salt. Grill (broil) about 7.5 cm/3 in below the heat for 4–5 minutes until the skin is crisp and dark. Remove from the grill, cover loosely with foil and leave to rest for 10 minutes.

Carve into thin slices. Add the pistachios to the relish and serve with the duck.

 It can be difficult to get the pomegranate seeds out of the skin without taking a lot of bitter white pith with them, so roll the pomegranate all over on a hard surface with the palm of your hand – not too firmly or you will squeeze the juice out of the seeds – and then cut it open; the seeds will come out far more easily.

Wild mushrooms with game is a classic seasonal combination, and the faint smokiness and sweetness of the wine add an extra layer of richness to the flavours.

Most large supermarkets now stock packets of mixed wild mushrooms in the autumn and winter, which are perfect for this dish, as each type of wild mushroom has its own particular texture and taste. Only wash the mushrooms if they are really gritty or earthy as some of their delicate flavour will inevitably disappear down the drain; I find the best way to clean them is to brush away any dirt or bits of vegetation with a soft toothbrush that I keep especially for this purpose.

Partridge can be fiddly to eat so do not hesitate to use your fingers.

roast partridge with wild mushrooms and marsala

15 g/¹/₂ oz dried porcini mushrooms

60 ml/4 tbsp olive oil

75 g/3 oz shallots, peeled and finely chopped

15 ml/1 tbsp fresh thyme leaves

200 g/7 oz wild mushrooms, cleaned and torn into pieces

150 ml/¹/₄ pint/²/₃ cup Marsala wine

200 ml/7 fl oz/scant 1 cup double (heavy) cream

Sea salt and freshly ground black pepper

2 partridges

150 g/5 oz pancetta or streaky bacon rashers (slices), rinded

Place the porcini mushrooms in a small bowl and cover with boiling water. Set aside to soak for 30 minutes.

Heat the oil in a small saucepan and add the shallots. Cook gently over a low heat until translucent. Raise the heat to medium, add the thyme and wild mushrooms, and cook for about 15 minutes until the mushrooms release their moisture and start to brown.

Pour in the Marsala, bring to the boil and let it bubble fiercely for a couple of minutes, then turn down to a simmer.

Strain the porcini mushrooms through a fine sieve (strainer), reserving the liquid. Roughly snip the porcini with scissors and add to the wild mushrooms in the saucepan. Stir in the soaking liquid, the cream and some seasoning and cook gently until thick.

While the sauce is cooking, preheat the oven to 220°C/425°F/gas 7/fan oven 200°C. Place the partridges in a roasting tin, season them well, cover the breasts with the pancetta or bacon and roast for 20 minutes. Push the pancetta or bacon to one side and cook for a further 10 minutes to brown the breasts. Remove from the oven, cover loosely with foil and set aside to rest for 10 minutes.

Place the partridges and bacon on warm two plates and pour the wild mushroom sauce around them.

Forget about mustard and ketchup, this aioli is the BEST sauce for sausages! And one of our favourite ways to eat them is in a warm baguette or ciabatta, rather like a hot dog: the aioli and the juices from the sausages both seep into the bread, softening the crust and mingling deliciously – messy, but terribly good.

There are as many best ways to cook sausages as there are cooks, but I have found that if I resist the temptation to Quickstep – to hurry them and urge them on – I end up with a burnished skin and a moist, juicy sausage.

sausages with roasted red pepper aioli

Sausages – as many as you fancy

15 ml/1 tbsp olive oil

1 quantity of Provençal Roasted Red Pepper Aioli (see page 64)

Heat the oil in a heavy-based frying pan and add the sausages. Cook them slowly over a low heat, turning them occasionally, until they are golden and caramelised.

Serve immediately with the aioli.

 In the summer, of course, just sling the sausages on the barbecue.

I came across proper Greek yoghurt many years ago, on a walking holiday in western Crete, long before the SNP's arrival on the scene and long before our supermarket shelves were lined not only with authentic Greek yoghurt made from sheep or goat milk, but also with countless other 'Greek-style' versions. In those days, I used to make my own yoghurt in a thermos flask, and it was invariably thin and mouth-puckering.

We 'rediscovered' it together more recently, on another walking holiday in Crete. We were in the White Mountains, taking a rest and drinking in the view. A grizzled old peasant, dressed in rusty black, shuffled along the mountain track, leading a donkey. When he reached us, he grinned toothlessly and asked: 'Yaourti?'. The panniers on each side of the donkey were laden with a motley collection of glass jars of yoghurt, their waxed paper covers held tightly in place with an elastic band. It was thick and creamy, with the faintest whiff of the farmyard and a yellow, wrinkled crust.

cretan meatballs with garlic and herb yoghurt

FOR THE MEATBALLS:

5 ml/1 tsp olive oil

30 g/1¼ oz wholemeal bread, without crusts

15 g/½ oz onion, coarsely chopped

15 g/½ oz fresh parsley, roughly chopped

400 g/14 oz minced (ground) lamb

1 egg

30 g/1¼ oz/scant ⅓ cup freshly grated Parmesan cheese

5 ml/1 tsp sea salt

FOR THE FRESH TOMATO SAUCE:

300 g/11 oz ripe tomatoes, roughly chopped

1 garlic clove, peeled

100 ml/3½ fl oz/scant 1½ cup olive oil

Sea salt and freshly ground black pepper

FOR THE YOGHURT:

250 ml/8 fl oz/1 cup Greek-style plain yoghurt

1 garlic clove, peeled and crushed

15 g/½ oz chopped fresh parsley

15 g/½ oz chopped fresh mint

30 ml/2 tbsp olive oil

Sea salt and freshly ground black pepper

TO SERVE:

Pitta bread

To make the meatballs, brush a gratin dish with the oil. Place the bread in a food processor and whiz to make coarse breadcrumbs. Add the onion and parsley and process until it is all fairly finely chopped.

Tip the mixture into a bowl and add the lamb, egg, Parmesan and salt. Now for the satisfyingly messy part! Using your hands, mix everything thoroughly, then roll it into meatballs about 3 cm/1¼ in in diameter. Place them in the prepared dish and set aside until you are ready.

To make the tomato sauce, place the tomatoes, garlic and oil in a food processor or blender and process to a fairly smooth puree. Don't worry about the bits of tomato skin – they won't be noticeable in the final dish. Season to taste.

Put the yoghurt in a small bowl and stir in the garlic, herbs, oil and seasoning to taste.

Preheat the oven to 200°C/400°F/gas 6/fan oven 180°C. Pour the tomato sauce over and around the meatballs and bake them uncovered for 15 minutes.

Serve with the yoghurt and some warm pitta bread.

 The meatballs can be prepared up to a day in advance and kept chilled.

The tomato sauce can be made several hours in advance. If it separates, beat it with a balloon whisk until it comes together again.

The inspiration for this dish is half Italian and half Lebanese, with a dash of soy sauce for good measure. It is a wonderful combination of flavours – the sparkling Mediterranean on a plate!

Countless versions of the aubergine purée, often referred to as 'poor man's caviare', are found throughout the Middle East; I often double or even triple the quantity as it is very versatile – another of my favourite uses for it is stuffed into warm pitta bread with Greek Salata with Fresh Herbs (page 20).

lamb chops with roast peppers and tomatoes

1 large aubergine (eggplant)

2 garlic cloves, peeled

100 ml/3¹/₂ fl oz/scant 1 cup olive oil

Sea salt and freshly ground black pepper

1 large red (bell) pepper, about 200 g/7 oz, seeded and cut into 1 cm/¹/₂ in wide strips

1 large yellow pepper, about 200 g/7 oz, seeded and cut into 1 cm/¹/₂ in wide strips

125 g/4¹/₂ oz red onions, peeled and sliced

2 sprigs of rosemary

5 ml/1 tsp soy sauce

Juice of ¹/₂ lemon

15 ml/1 tbsp dark tahini

150 g/5 oz cherry tomatoes

4 lamb chops

30 ml/2 tbsp basil, cut into strips with scissors

Heat the oven to 200°C/400°F/gas 6/fan oven 180°C.

Peel the aubergine, cut it into 1 cm/¹/₂ in chunks and place in a roasting tray with the garlic. Drizzle over 45 ml/3 tbsp of the olive oil and season to taste. Cook on the top shelf of the oven for 30 minutes until tender.

Mix the peppers, onions and rosemary in one layer in a large roasting tray. Drizzle with the remaining oil, season well and place on the lower shelf of the oven until the aubergines are done and then transfer them to the top shelf. Cook for a further 30 minutes, stirring once or twice.

Scrape the aubergine and garlic mixture into a food processor, add the soy sauce, lemon juice and tahini and process to a smooth purée. Adjust the seasoning and set aside.

Mix the cherry tomatoes into the peppers and cook for a further 10 minutes until the peppers are blackened a bit along the edges and the tomatoes are soft.

Heat the grill (broiler) to high. Season the chops, place in the grill pan and cook about 2.5 cm/1 in from the heat for about 3 minutes on each side if you like your lamb pink, 5 minutes for better done.

To serve, divide the pepper mixture between two warm plates, top with the lamb chops, spoon some aubergine purée on the side and sprinkle with the basil.

This salad can be prepared several days ahead – the flavour improves with keeping – but don't add the sugar snaps until you are ready to eat as they will lose their bright colour. Sprinkle the cashews on just before serving to keep them crisp and crunchy.

thai beef salad with sugar snap peas

120 ml/4 fl oz/½ cup toasted sesame oil

200 g/7 oz rump or fillet steak

200 g/7 oz onions, peeled and thickly sliced

1 large red chilli, seeded and sliced

90 ml/6 tbsp soy sauce

100 g/4 oz button mushrooms

1 garlic clove, peeled

15 ml/1 tbsp cider vinegar

15 ml/1 tbsp honey

30 ml/2 tbsp peanut butter

100 g/4 oz sugar snap peas

50 g/2 oz/½ cup roasted cashew nuts

15 ml/1 tbsp chopped fresh coriander (cilantro)

Heat 15 ml/1 tbsp of the oil in a frying pan, add the steak and cook for about 3 minutes on each side. Remove and set aside on a plate to cool.

Pour another 15 ml/1 tbsp of the oil into the pan and add the onions and chilli. Stir-fry for about 5 minutes until the onions are translucent but still retain some crunch. Remove from the pan and place in a mixing bowl.

Add another 30 ml/2 tbsp of the oil and 30 ml/2 tbsp of the soy sauce to the pan and bring to the boil. Add the mushrooms and cook for 10 minutes, stirring occasionally, until they have absorbed the soy sauce and are nicely browned. Transfer them to the bowl with the onions.

To make the dressing, place the garlic, remaining soy sauce, cider vinegar and honey in a food processor or a blender and process briefly. With the motor running, slowly pour the remaining sesame oil through the tube, then add the peanut butter – the mixture will thicken to the consistency of single (light) cream.

When the beef is cool, slice it thinly, add it to the onions and mushrooms, pour the dressing over and mix gently. Cover and chill.

Cook the sugar snap peas in salted boiling water for 3 minutes, cool under cold running water and drain well.

When you are ready to eat, mix the sugar snap peas into the beef. Transfer everything to a serving bowl and scatter the cashews and coriander over the top.

 The sugar snap peas can be cooked up to 24 hours in advance and chilled. Add them to the salad just before eating.

I have no idea who Jansson was but am grateful to him – or her – for this wonderfully savoury gratin flavoured with anchovies. It is very, very rich, I admit, but the texture and flavour are incomparable.

The magic of this dish is the contrast between the luscious, indulgent, mellow gratin and the sharp, aromatic, vibrant salsa. We have this on its own for supper – often when we feel the need for comfort and a treat! – but I also love serving it with a leg of lamb or a plain roast chicken. I know it sounds like a lot of potato for two people but it cooks right down.

jansson's temptation with salsa verde

FOR THE POTATOES:

500 g/18 oz potatoes, peeled and thinly sliced

Sea salt and freshly ground black pepper

2 garlic cloves, peeled and thinly sliced

4 large anchovy fillets, snipped into 1 cm/$^1/_2$ in lengths with scissors

250 ml/8 fl oz/1 cup double (heavy) cream

FOR THE SALSA:

1 garlic clove, peeled

15 g/$^1/_2$ oz fresh parsley, coarsely chopped

15 g/$^1/_2$ oz fresh mint, coarsely chopped

2 spring onions (scallions), sliced

4 anchovy fillets, snipped into 1 cm/$^1/_2$ in lengths with scissors

30 ml/2 tbsp capers, rinsed and squeezed dry

10 green olives, stoned (pitted)

250 ml/8 fl oz/1 cup olive oil

Sea salt and freshly ground black pepper

Lemon juice

To make the potatoes, cook the slices in salted boiling water for 5 minutes. Drain and set aside until cool enough to handle.

Layer up the potato slices in a small gratin dish, seasoning and sprinkling with garlic and anchovies as you go. Pour the cream over it all and bake in the oven at 200°C/400°F/gas 6/fan oven 180°C for 1 hour until the top is golden-brown.

Meanwhile, to make the salsa, place all the ingredients except the lemon juice in a food processor and process until smooth. Check the seasoning and sharpen with lemon juice to taste – it needs to have a good bite.

Serve the potatoes with the salsa.

 If you are not wildly keen on anchovies, the recipe also works well with a couple of rashers (slices) of streaky bacon, grilled (broiled) until crisp.

Not to be confused with the Moroccan tagine, which is a stew, the Tunisian tagine is a baked egg dish, similar to an Italian frittata or Spanish tortilla. It can be made with vegetables such as courgettes (zucchini), peppers, aubergines (eggplants), peas or green beans, and served as part of a mezze with salads; or it can contain meat or cheese. We have also had it topped with a spicy tomato sauce.

tunisian tagine méchouia

250 g/9 oz tomatoes, quartered

1 large red (bell) pepper, about 200 g/7 oz

15 ml/1 tbsp olive oil

125 g/4½ oz onions, peeled and coarsely chopped

1 garlic clove, peeled and sliced

250 g/9 oz sausages, casings removed

Sea salt and freshly ground black pepper

3 eggs, beaten

50 g/2 oz/½ cup freshly grated Cheddar (Monterey Jack) cheese

Preheat the oven to 200°C/400°F/gas 6/fan oven 180°C. Place the tomatoes on a baking (cookie) sheet lined with baking parchment and roast them for 1 hour until slightly shrivelled and starting to blacken along the edges.

While the tomatoes are cooking, heat the grill (broiler) to high, place the red pepper in a roasting tray and grill (broil) about 4 cm/1½ in from the heat until it is black and blistered all over. Allow to cool, then peel it, remove the stem and seeds and cut the flesh into 1cm/½ in pieces.

Heat the oil in a frying pan, add the onion and garlic and cook for 10 minutes until translucent. Add the sausagemeat and some seasoning and continue to cook for 15 minutes, stirring occasionally and breaking down any lumps with the back of a wooden spoon.

Stir in the tomatoes and red pepper. Allow to cool slightly, then add the eggs. Pour the mixture into an ovenproof china dish, sprinkle with the cheese and cook at 200°C/400°F/gas 6/fan oven 180°C for about 40 minutes until it is firm to the touch and the top is golden.

Serve hot or cold.

 This is delicious cold and makes really good picnic food.

This is a delicately flavoured purée, with the sweet richness of the garlic decidedly in the background but still very much present. It goes beautifully with roast lamb or chicken and makes a comfortable bed for a couple of poached eggs. I always like to sieve it through a mouli-légumes to get rid of any of the stray whiskers that celeriac tends to have but, if you are not bothered, you can Quickstep through this recipe.

celeriac and roast garlic purée

900 g/2 lb celeriac (celery root), peeled and cut into 2 cm/³/₄ in chunks

30 ml/2 tbsp olive oil

Sea salt and freshly ground black pepper

15 garlic cloves, peeled

60 ml/4 tbsp double (heavy) cream

Preheat the oven to 200°C/400°F/gas 6/fan oven 180°C.

Place the celeriac in a roasting tin, drizzle with the oil and season to taste. Transfer to the oven and roast, stirring once, for 30 minutes.

Add the whole garlic cloves and cook for a further 30 minutes, by which time the celeriac and garlic should be soft and golden.

Scrape into a food processor, add the cream and process until smooth. Strain through the medium disc of a mouli-légumes.

Check the seasoning, then serve immediately.

It seems impossible to find the perfect, juicy nectarine. They are usually rock hard when bought and start to deteriorate long before they ripen. But cooking them in a pie or crumble softens them and brings out their summer magic.

sweet nectarine crumble tarts

30 g/1¼ oz soft brown sugar

40 g/1¾ oz wholemeal flour

30 g/1¼ oz unsalted (sweet) butter

30 g/1¼ oz chopped walnuts

Ready rolled puff pastry (paste)

2 large nectarines, as ripe as possible

TO SERVE:

Thick cream

To make the crumble topping, place the sugar, flour, butter and walnuts in a food processor and process until the mixture resembles soft breadcrumbs. Set aside or chill overnight.

Preheat the oven to 200°C/400°F/gas 6/fan oven 180°C.

Cut two rounds, about 13 cm/5 in in diameter, from the puff pastry and place them on a baking (cookie) sheet.

Cut the nectarines in half, remove the stones and slice the flesh into half-moon slices about 3 mm/⅛ in thick. Arrange the slices on the pastry rounds, leaving a 1 cm/½ in edge. Carefully spoon the crumble topping over the fruit.

Bake for about 25 minutes until the topping is golden and the nectarines are just starting to release their juices.

Using a spatula, transfer the tarts to two warm plates. Serve immediately with plenty of cream.

Stoning cherries can be fiddly and you end up with stained fingernails, but they are incredibly delicious when lightly poached in this Cassis syrup so they are well worth the trouble.

I came across the idea of sweet and savoury filo crisps in an American food magazine a long time ago and find them wonderfully versatile – certainly easier and quicker than making biscuits, and I love the texture.

warm cherries in cassis syrup with filo crisps

FOR THE CRISPS:

2 sheets of filo pastry (paste), about 30 x 18 cm/12 x 7 in

15 g/½ oz/1 tbsp unsalted (sweet) butter, melted

10 ml/2 tsp caster (superfine) sugar

15 g/½ oz/2 tbsp skinned, toasted hazelnuts (filberts), chopped

FOR THE CHERRIES:

45 ml/3 tbsp caster (superfine) sugar

45 ml/3 tbsp Cassis

30 ml/2 tbsp water

400 g/14 oz cherries, stoned (pitted)

20 g/¾ oz unsalted (sweet) butter

TO SERVE:

Thick cream

Preheat the oven to 200°C/400°F/gas 6/180°C.

To make the crisps, lay one sheet of filo pastry out on a work surface (keep the other covered with a tea towel (dish cloth) as filo dries out very quickly). Cut the sheet in half into two squares. Brush one with melted butter and sprinkle it liberally with sugar and hazelnuts. Place the second square on top of the first, brush again with butter and sprinkle with sugar and nuts. Repeat with the second sheet of pastry so that you have four layers. Press down lightly to stick the layers together and cut into four triangles.

Using a spatula, carefully transfer the triangles to a baking (cookie) sheet and bake for about 10 minutes until lightly golden. Remove from the oven and leave to cool.

To make the cherries, put the sugar, Cassis and water in a small saucepan and bring to the boil, stirring all the time. Cook for 2 minutes, then add the cherries. Carefully turn them over and over in the syrup until they are hot and start to release their juices. Take the pan off the heat and add the butter, swirling it around to melt it.

Serve the cherries immediately with the crisps and plenty of cream.

 You can use raspberries or blackberries instead of cherries if you prefer – just be very careful not to overcook them or you will have berry soup before you realise it.

the waltz

The dance I would associate with this section is the modern, slow-tempo waltz rather than the twirling and spinning Viennese style. Modern waltz has a wonderfully flowing movement to it, with a rhythmic sway and lilt, an easy swing into the turns, a graceful rise from the heel to the toes. It may require a certain degree of method and control, but its overall feel is comfortable and laid-back. This is how it should feel with the recipes in this chapter, recipes for the hassle- and stress-free times when you are not pushing and rushing through your life, when you are not bothered if things take longer than expected, and you can capture real pleasure in the slowness. Weekends are the obvious setting for these *repas de deux*, but the Waltz need not be confined to Saturdays and Sundays. You can dance it on days when, for example:

◆ you are treating yourself to a half-day off
◆ a friend has just cancelled a day out together
◆ the trains aren't running due to an impromptu strike
◆ the car won't start and the garage can't send a mechanic until late afternoon
◆ you have to stay at home to wait for the washing machine repair man
◆ you had planned a day at the beach but it is pouring with rain
◆ the tutors all have food poisoning and lectures are postponed until further notice
◆ the information you need to complete the project hasn't arrived and you can do nothing further until it turns up
◆ your computer seems to have caught a virus
◆ it's your birthday and today you are going to please yourself

The Waltz takes as long as it takes. Some of these *repas de deux* recipes will take barely longer than the Foxtrot; others are more time-consuming. But all of them involve leisure, relaxation, and that elusive and precious feeling that you have at least sufficient time, if not all the time in the world. Then the creative process can sway and lilt, swing and turn, rise and fall. It doesn't matter if something needs to cool before the next step can be undertaken; or if it has to cook for three hours; or marinate for six. And when you eventually sit down to eat, you can savour the fruits of a couple of hours, or even a day, dancing to a different tune and living in the moment.

Pungent, rich, garlicky heaven! Its strength and power can be slightly tamed by using a younger or older goats' cheese, according to taste – I prefer a fresh cheese but, if you like cheeses with a hint of the stable, go for something more mature.

This aioli is wonderful dolloped into vegetables soups; with new potatoes roasted in olive oil, chopped rosemary and grated Parmesan cheese; with grilled (broiled) chicken marinated in chilli, lime juice and spices; and folded into a warm salad of chick peas (garbanzos), red onions, olives and sun-dried tomatoes.

roasted garlic and goats' cheese aioli

1 whole head of garlic, separated into cloves

2 egg yolks

Sea salt and freshly ground black pepper

100 ml/3½ fl oz/scant ½ cup olive oil

100 g/4 oz goats' cheese

100 ml/3½ fl oz/scant ½ cup plain yoghurt

15 g/½ oz basil

Preheat the oven to 200°C/400°F/gas 6/fan oven 180°C.

Place the unpeeled garlic in a ramekin (custard cup) or a small baking dish, wrap it well in foil and cook in the oven for 1 hour until it is soft. Allow to cool, then peel.

Meanwhile, to make the mayonnaise base, place the egg yolks and some seasoning in the bowl of a food processor and whiz up. With the motor still running, slowly pour in the oil, then add the cheese and finally the yoghurt. Add the peeled garlic and the basil, check the seasoning and whiz again.

 The aioli can be made up to 48 hours in advance – any longer and it starts taking over the whole show.

See also Black Bean Soup with Roasted Garlic and Cheese Aioli (page 120) and Roasted Tomatoes with Garlic and Goats' Cheese Aioli (page 131).

Add some aromatic herbs to the Roasted Tomatoes on page 131 and you have an incredibly versatile sauce that freezes well and can be used for pasta, fried eggs, grilled (broiled) sausages, fish or chicken, oven-roasted Mediterranean vegetables or to flavour a stew. It is also my favourite sauce for meatballs.

roasted tomato sauce with honey and herbs

makes about 500 ml/17 fl oz/2¼ cups

1 kg/2¼ lb tomatoes, halved

6 large garlic cloves, peeled and thinly sliced

15 ml/1 tbsp runny honey

30 ml/2 tbsp olive oil

Sea salt and freshly ground black pepper

A handful of aromatic herb sprigs such as thyme, rosemary or oregano

Preheat the oven to 200°C/400°F/gas 6/fan oven 180°C.

Put the tomato halves, cut-sides up, in a roasting tray lined with baking parchment and push the garlic slivers into the seedy bits. Drizzle first with the honey and then the oil. Season well and strew the herbs on top.

Cook in the oven for 1–1½ hours until soft and slightly blackened. Allow to cool slightly, discard the herbs and process in a blender or food processor until smooth. You can sieve (strain) it if you want but I don't bother.

Although I have in the past made this tapenade with sun-dried tomatoes, I find that roasting fresh tomatoes long enough to concentrate their flavour but still leave them with some moistness results in a fresher, rounder sauce.

This tapenade is wonderful in a toasted cheese sandwich, with a creamy vegetable gratin such as potato, root vegetable or celery, and with any combination of Italian cured meat, such as prosciutto, salami, coppa or mortadella.

roasted fresh tomato tapenade

500 g/18 oz tomatoes, halved

30 ml/2 tbsp olive oil

5 ml/1 tsp dried oregano

Sea salt and freshly ground black pepper

2 garlic cloves, peeled

3 anchovy fillets

8 black olives, stoned (pitted)

15 ml/1 tbsp capers, rinsed

15 g/¹/₂ oz basil

100 ml/3¹/₂ fl oz/scant ¹/₂ cup olive oil

Preheat the oven to 150°C/300°F/gas 2/fan oven 135°C.

Arrange the tomato halves, cut-sides up, in a roasting tin lined with baking parchment. Drizzle the oil over them and sprinkle with the oregano, a little salt and some pepper. Bake in the oven for 2 hours. Allow to cool.

Place the tomatoes in the bowl of a food processor with all the other ingredients and process to a fairly smooth purée. Taste for seasoning – it is unlikely you will need any more salt as the anchovies are salty.

The tapenade benefits from sitting for a few hours, to mellow and blend the flavours. It will keep, covered, in the fridge for up to 3 days; after that it gets decidedly assertive.

See also Penne with Roasted Vegetables and Tomato Tapenade (page 173) and Roast Chicken with Roasted Tomato Tapenade (page 156).

This soup, just like the Black Bean Cakes with Mango Tabbouleh on page 124, needs a bit of forward planning as the beans require a couple of hours of cooking. But they need no attention and can be done several days ahead if that suits you better, and the soup itself matures well in the fridge. Red kidney beans also work well in this recipe, but then you lose the dramatic colour combination.

black bean soup with roasted garlic and goats' cheese aioli

250 g/9 oz black beans, rinsed

1 bay leaf

5 ml/1 tsp cumin seeds

30 ml/2 tbsp olive oil

250 g/9 oz onions, peeled and coarsely chopped

1 hot red or green chilli, seeded and sliced

15 ml/1 tbsp bouillon powder

Sea salt and freshly ground black pepper

10 g/scant 1/2 oz fresh coriander (cilantro), coarsely chopped

FOR THE SALSA:

125 g/4 1/2 oz cherry tomatoes, quartered

2 spring onions (scallions), thinly sliced

1 garlic clove, crushed

30 ml/2 tbsp olive oil

15 ml/1 tbsp chopped fresh coriander (cilantro)

Sea salt and freshly ground black pepper

TO SERVE:

1 quantity of Roasted Garlic and Goats' Cheese Aioli (see page 116)

Put the beans in a saucepan with the bay leaf, cover with water and simmer gently for at least 2 hours until soft. Allow to cool slightly.

Toast the cumin seeds in a small pan over a medium heat until they are aromatic – stand over them because this will take only a couple minutes and they will burn in a trice and be bitter; all you are aiming for is a whiff of spice. Place them in a mortar or spice grinder and grind them to a coarse powder.

Heat the oil in a medium saucepan, add the onions and cook, stirring occasionally, for about 20 minutes until soft and golden.

Add the chilli and cook for 5 minutes, then add the cumin and cook for 2 more minutes.

Scrape it all into a food processor. Add the cooled beans, the bouillon powder and some seasoning and process to a medium-smooth purée. Return it to the saucepan and reheat. Check the seasoning.

The salsa is best made fairly close to serving time as it tends to go soggy, so have the separate elements prepared and ready and then just mix and season them at the last minute.

Ladle the soup into two warm bowls, sprinkle with the coriander and serve with the aioli and salsa.

provençal butter bean salad with baked goats' cheese

200 g/7 oz cherry tomatoes, halved

1 small red (bell) pepper, about 150 g/5 oz

1 small yellow pepper, about 150 g/5 oz

65 g/2½ oz red onion, peeled and finely chopped

1 garlic clove, peeled and crushed

60 ml/4 tbsp olive oil, plus extra for drizzling

15 ml/1 tbsp Tabasco sauce

1 x 400 g/14 oz/large can of butter (lima) beans, drained and rinsed

Sea salt and freshly ground black pepper

30 g/1¼ oz/generous ½ cup wholemeal breadcrumbs

15 ml/1 tbsp fresh thyme leaves

1 egg, beaten

2 x 100 g/4 oz round goats' cheeses

30 ml/2 tbsp chopped fresh parsley or basil

Preheat the oven to 220°C/450°F/gas 7/fan oven 200°C. Place the tomatoes on a baking (cookie) sheet lined with baking parchment and roast them for 30 minutes until slightly shrivelled and starting to blacken along the edges.

While the tomatoes are cooking, heat the grill (broiler) to high and grill (broil) the peppers 10 cm/4 in from the heat, turning them every so often, until they are black and blistered all over. Allow to cool, then remove the skin, seeds and stalk and cut the flesh into 1 cm/½ in wide strips.

Place the peppers in a roomy bowl with the onion, garlic, oil, Tabasco, beans and some seasoning.

Place the breadcrumbs and thyme leaves in a small shallow bowl and drizzle a little oil over them. Toss them around with a spoon to distribute the oil.

Using a pastry brush, paint the beaten egg all over the goats' cheeses – a bit of a messy business! – then roll them in the breadcrumbs, coating them thoroughly. Place on a baking sheet lined with baking parchment.

When the tomatoes are ready, add them to the rest of the salad ingredients and mix together gently.

Reduce the oven temperature to 200°C/400°F/gas 6/fan oven 180°C, put the cheeses on the middle shelf and bake for 10 minutes.

Divide the salad between two plates. Carefully lift the cheeses off the baking sheet with a spatula – don't worry if they collapse a bit – and place on top of the butter bean salad. Sprinkle the parsley or basil over everything and eat immediately while the cheese is still beautifully gooey.

The contrasts and layers of flavours in this dish are guaranteed to pep up the most jaded palate: rich and spicy beans, aromatic mint, sweet mango, sharp thick yoghurt. If you really cannot be bothered to cook the beans, you can use a can of red kidney beans with a fair degree of success but it just won't have the same impact – so why spoil a fantastic dish for the sake of a bit of organisation? The beans are easy to cook the day before and take care of themselves.

black bean cakes with mango tabbouleh

175 g/6 oz black beans, rinsed

1 bay leaf

60 ml/4 tbsp olive oil

150 g/5 oz onions, peeled and coarsely chopped

2 garlic cloves, peeled and crushed

7.5 ml/1½ tsp cumin seeds

Sea salt and freshly ground black pepper

15 ml/1 tbsp chipotle chilli sauce (available from delicatessens and the speciality section of large supermarkets)

1 egg

FOR THE TABBOULEH:

250 ml/8 fl oz/1 cup water

Sea salt and freshly ground black pepper

125 g/4½ oz/generous 1 cup bulghar (cracked wheat)

50 g/2 oz red onion, peeled and finely chopped

1 garlic clove, peeled and crushed

50 g/2 oz fresh mint, coarsely chopped

1 small mango, peeled and cut into 1 cm/½ in dice

30 ml/2 tbsp olive oil

TO SERVE:

250 ml/8 fl oz/1 cup Greek-style plain yoghurt, seasoned

Place the beans in a saucepan with the bay leaf, cover with water, bring to the boil, cover and simmer gently for about 2 hours until soft. Pour into a sieve (strainer) and leave to drain for at least 30 minutes. (All of this can be done the day, or even several days, before.)

Heat half the oil in a frying pan, add the onions and garlic and cook gently, stirring occasionally, for about 20 minutes until soft and golden.

Place the cumin seeds in a small heavy-based pan and toast them, stirring over a medium heat, until aromatic. Tip them into a mortar or spice grinder and grind coarsely.

When the onions and garlic are ready, stir in some seasoning, the cumin and chipotle sauce and cook for 1 minute. Remove from the heat.

Place the drained black beans in a food processor with the egg and process, stopping often to scrape down the sides of the bowl, until you have a medium-coarse paste with chunks of bean in it. Scrape the beans into the frying pan with the onion mixture and mix well. Check the seasoning.

Shape the mixture into four cakes – a pastry (paste) ring is a tremendous asset here! Place on a plate or baking (cookie) sheet and chill for at least 30 minutes to firm up.

Make the tabbouleh about 15 minutes before you intend to fry the bean cakes. Bring the water to the boil in a medium saucepan, add some seasoning and stir in the bulghar. Cover and remove from the heat. Let it sit for 20 minutes, by which time it will have absorbed the water and softened. Stir in the remaining tabbouleh ingredients.

Heat the remaining olive oil in a heavy-based frying pan and cook the bean cakes for about 10 minutes on each side.

To serve, divide the tabbouleh between two warm plates and top with two black bean cakes each and some seasoned yoghurt.

 You could, if you're short of time, use 5 ml/1 tsp of ground cumin instead of seeds and skip the toasting and grinding. However, do use the seeds if at all possible as the flavour of toasted, freshly ground spices is in a totally different league.

You will need two china ramekins (custard cups) and individual gratin dishes for this recipe.

Soufflés have a bad reputation: capricious, moody, fickle, unmerciful, and with a distinct 'don't mess with me' attitude – definitely not the kind of thing a busy cook cares to trifle with! However, bake your soufflé twice and the stress and anxiety connected with its rise and fall vanishes. A twice-baked soufflé, unlike its dreaded sibling, the 'rush-from-the-oven-to-the-table-before-it-collapses' soufflé, is friendly, amenable and forgiving: not only will it rise up again like magic on its second baking, but it will also hold its airy volume for more than long enough to be served in comfort. Admittedly, it doesn't billow up to quite such dizzy heights as a normal soufflé – it must be resilient enough to withstand unmoulding – but its texture is just as light and ethereal. See also Twice-baked Muscat Raisin and Chocolate Soufflés (page 182).

twice-baked smoked salmon soufflés with orange salsa

FOR THE SOUFFLÉS:

20 g/³/₄ oz butter, plus extra for greasing

20 g/³/₄ oz/3 tbsp plain (all-purpose) flour

120 ml/4 fl oz/¹/₂ cup milk

75 g/3 oz smoked salmon, diced

30 ml/2 tbsp finely chopped fresh dill (dill weed)

2 large eggs, separated

Sea salt and freshly ground black pepper

A pinch of cream of tartar

120 ml/4 fl oz/¹/₂ cup double (heavy) cream

FOR THE SALSA:

15 g/¹/₂ oz fresh dill (dill weed)

Grated zest and juice of 1 large orange

1 garlic clove, peeled

15 ml/1 tbsp capers, rinsed and squeezed dry

100 ml/3¹/₂ fl oz/scant ¹/₂ cup olive oil

25 g/1 oz/¹/₄ cup freshly grated Parmesan cheese

Sea salt and freshly ground black pepper

1 large hard-boiled (hard-cooked) egg, peeled

A squeeze of lemon juice (optional)

To make the soufflés, melt the butter in a small saucepan over a medium heat. Stir in the flour and cook, stirring, for a few minutes until the mixture looks like wet sand.

Slowly whisk in the milk and bring to the boil, stirring all the time. Reduce the heat and simmer for a couple of minutes. Allow to cool slightly, then stir in the salmon, dill and egg yolks. Season well with pepper and some salt – you will not need much as the smoked salmon is salty but bear in mind that, once the egg whites have been incorporated, the flavour will be weaker. Set aside to cool completely.

Preheat the oven to 200°C/400°F/gas 6/fan oven 180°C. Grease two 250 ml/ 8 fl oz/1 cup china ramekins (custard cups) and line the bases with a round of baking parchment.

Whisk the egg whites with the cream of tartar until stiff and fold gently into the soufflé base. Divide the mixture between the prepared ramekins.

Place the ramekins in a roasting tin half-filled with hot water and bake for 25 minutes until well risen and lightly browned. Remove the dishes from the water bath and allow to cool. (The soufflés can be prepared up to this point and chilled for 24 hours; bring them back to room temperature before the second bake.)

To make the salsa, place the dill, orange zest and juice, garlic and capers in a food processor and pulse to break it all down a bit. With the motor still running, add the oil, Parmesan and some seasoning and process until smooth. Add the egg and pulse just enough to chop it coarsely – you are looking for a green sauce flecked with yellow and white. Transfer to a bowl and check the seasoning. Add a squeeze of lemon juice if it tastes a bit bland – it will depend on the sweetness of the orange. (The salsa can be prepared up to 3 hours ahead of time but any longer and it will start to lose its fresh colour and flavour.)

Preheat the oven to 200°C/400°F/gas 6/fan oven 180°C. Unmould the soufflés by carefully running a small knife around the inside and turning them out on to the palm of your hand – be very gentle as they are delicate! Remove the baking parchment and place them, browned-sides up, in two gratin dishes about 13 cm/5 in across. (A single one large enough to hold them both with 3 cm/1¼ in between each will work, though they will be a little more difficult to serve.)

Pour the cream over the soufflés, then bake them for 20 minutes until they have puffed up again and the cream is bubbling and starting to brown. Serve immediately with the salsa.

While the smoked salmon soufflé on page 126 is a distinctly northern belle, its flavours fresh, light and elegant, this cheese soufflé is without doubt a Mediterrranean signorina – predictably bold and sassy, its flavours sunny, vibrant and lingering.

If, having tried this Parmesan and goats' cheese version, you fancy expanding your cheese soufflé repertoire, a strong Cheddar cheese with some garlic and herb Boursin is another successful combination – serve it with Green Olive and Oregano Tapenade (page 18) instead of pesto and you have a Provençal demoiselle.

You will need two china ramekins (custard cups) and individual gratin dishes for this recipe.

twice-baked cheese soufflés with tomatoes and pesto

FOR THE TOMATOES:

150 g/5 oz ripe tomatoes, halved if small or quartered if large

Sea salt and freshly ground black pepper

5 ml/1 tsp runny honey

15 ml/1 tbsp olive oil

FOR THE SOUFFLÉS:

20 g/$^3/_4$ oz butter, plus extra for greasing

20 g/$^3/_4$ oz/3 tbsp plain (all-purpose) flour

120 ml/4 fl oz/$^1/_2$ cup milk

Sea salt and freshly ground black pepper

Freshly grated nutmeg

50 g/2 oz/$^1/_2$ cup freshly grated Parmesan cheese

70 g/2$^3/_4$ oz goats' cheese

2 large eggs, separated

A pinch of cream of tartar

120 ml/4 fl oz/$^1/_2$ cup double (heavy) cream

FOR THE PESTO:

1 garlic clove, peeled

20 g/$^3/_4$ oz fresh basil

50 g/2 oz/$^1/_2$ cup freshly grated Parmesan cheese

120 ml/4 fl oz/$^1/_2$ cup olive oil

Start with the tomatoes as they can be prepared up to 24 hours beforehand and chilled. Preheat the oven to 200°C/400°F/gas 6/fan oven 180°C. Place the tomatoes, cut-sides up, on a baking (cookie) sheet lined with baking parchment. Season them well, then drizzle first with the honey and then the oil. Place them on the middle shelf of the oven and cook for about 1 hour until they are soft, slightly shrivelled and just starting to blacken along the edges.

To make the soufflés, melt the butter in a small saucepan over a medium heat. Stir in the flour and cook, stirring, for a few minutes until the mixture looks like wet sand.

Slowly whisk in the milk and bring to the boil, stirring all the time. Reduce the heat and simmer for a couple of minutes. Allow to cool slightly, then stir in 2.5 ml/½ tsp salt, some pepper, a little nutmeg, 35 g/1½ oz of the Parmesan, the goats' cheese and the egg yolks. Set aside to cool completely.

Preheat the oven to 200°C/400°F/gas 6/fan oven 180°C. Grease two 250 ml/ 8 fl oz/1 cup china ramekins (custard cups) and line the bases with a round of baking parchment.

Whisk the egg whites with the cream of tartar until stiff and fold gently into the soufflé base. Divide the mixture between the prepared ramekins.

Place the ramekins in a roasting tin half-filled with hot water and bake for 25 minutes on the top shelf of the oven until well risen and lightly browned. Remove the dishes from the water bath and allow to cool. (The soufflés can be prepared up to this point and chilled for 24 hours; bring them back to room temperature before the second bake.)

To make the pesto, place all the ingredients in a food processor and process until smooth. (The pesto will keep well in the refrigerator for several days.)

Preheat the oven to 200°C/400°F/gas 6/fan oven 180°C. Unmould the soufflés by carefully running a small knife around the inside and turning them out on to the palm of your hand – be very gentle as they are delicate! Remove the baking parchment and place them, browned-sides up, in two gratin dishes about 13 cm/5 in across. (A single one large enough to hold them both with 3 cm/1¼ in between each will work, though they will be a little more difficult to serve.)

Pour the cream over the soufflés, strew the remaining Parmesan over the tops and arrange the roasted tomatoes around. Bake them for 20 minutes until they have puffed up again and the cream is bubbling and starting to brown.

Serve immediately with the pesto.

We first discovered Catalán food when we spent four exciting days in Barcelona celebrating the SNP's birthday, and ate ourselves into an absolute stupor. The tapas bars are incredibly atmospheric – crowded, shadowy and exuberantly noisy – and serve outstanding food. Origens 99.9% in the La Ribera district was our favourite bar and we came across this Catalán onion pizza there.

It is reminiscent of the *pissaladière* of Provence. The flavours are beautifully simple and clean, and the contrast between the crisp, crunchy base and the sweet soft onions is a delight. A glass of chilled cava is the perfect accompaniment.

I put the anchovies on near the end of the coca's time in the oven to keep them plump and juicy – they go rather powdery if they are cooked for too long. If you prefer, you can make one larger coca, but I love plenty of crusty outer edge!

You can serve the coca straight from the oven, but it is also delicious cold and makes a wonderful picnic lunch on a long winter's walk – it really keeps out the cold somehow!

coca de cebolla catalana

FOR THE BASE:

200 g/7 oz/1¾ cups strong wholemeal (bread) flour, plus extra for dusting

6.5 ml/1¼ tsp/½ sachet easy-blend dried yeast

1.5 ml/¼ tsp sugar

2.5 ml/½ tsp sea salt

15 ml/1 tbsp olive oil

Warm water

FOR THE TOPPING:

45 ml/3 tbsp olive oil, plus extra for greasing

700 g/1½ lb onions, peeled and thinly sliced

15 ml/1 tbsp fresh thyme leaves

Sea salt and freshly ground black pepper

4 large anchovy fillets

To make the base, place the flour, yeast, sugar and salt in a roomy bowl and stir well with a wooden spoon. Drizzle the oil over everything and add just enough warm water to make a soft but not sticky dough – you will need about 150 ml/¼ pint/⅔ cup.

Stir briskly with the spoon until the dough comes together, then turn it out on to a work surface and knead for 5–10 minutes until smooth and elastic. Add a little more flour if it is too sticky. Place the dough in a bowl, dust the top with flour, cover with a damp tea towel (dish cloth) and leave to rise in a warm place for 1 hour, or overnight in the refrigerator.

Prepare the topping while the dough is rising. Heat the oil in a frying pan, add the onions, thyme and plenty of seasoning and cook over a gentle heat, stirring occasionally, for about 45 minutes until soft and golden. Allow to cool slightly.

Preheat the oven to 200°C/400°F/gas 6/fan oven 180°C. Divide the dough into two. Roll out each piece on a floured work surface into two thin rounds. Transfer to a lightly oiled baking (cookie) sheet and cover with the onions.

Bake for 15 minutes, then remove from the oven and arrange the anchovy fillets in a cross on top of the onions. Return to the oven and bake for a further 7 minutes.

Grilled (broiled) tomatoes on toast are one of the SNP's stand-bys and, however lacklustre the tomatoes may be to start with, by the time he has finished with them they are utterly delicious. We often have them as a quick lunch dish, particularly if there is any kind of leftover pesto or aioli sitting in the refrigerator.

Roasting the tomatoes takes longer but requires less attention, and makes them incredibly soft and luscious.

The roasted tomatoes also make a fabulous sauce (see page 117).

The ones my organic farmer delivers tend to be the size of a small apple and take about 1½ hours; if yours are smaller, they may be ready more quickly.

roasted tomatoes with garlic and goats' cheese aioli

500 g/18 oz tomatoes, halved

3 large garlic cloves, peeled and thinly sliced

10 ml/2 tsp runny honey

30 ml/2 tbsp olive oil

Sea salt and freshly ground black pepper

1 quantity of Roasted Garlic and Goats' Cheese Aioli (see page 116)

TO SERVE:

Bread

Preheat the oven to 200°C/400°F/gas 6/fan oven 180°C.

Put the tomatoes in a roasting tin lined with baking parchment and push the garlic slivers into the seedy bits. Drizzle first with the honey and then the oil. Season well, then cook for 1–1½ hours until soft and slightly blackened.

Serve warm with the aioli and plenty of fresh bread to mop up the juices.

The perfect brunch dish and a spring variation on the classic Eggs Benedict immortalised by Brennan's Restaurant in New Orleans. Needless to say, make this only in the spring, when you can buy local asparagus.

Although it all looks rather lengthy and complicated, it is actually easy to prepare and everything will sit quite happily if necessary while you sort yourself out: the brioche and asparagus can keep warm in the oven, the eggs in the frying pan, and the sauce over a pan of hot – not boiling – water.

asparagus eggs benedict with orange hollandaise

1 bunch of green asparagus

15 ml/1 tbsp olive oil

Sea salt and freshly ground black pepper

4 slices of brioche, toasted

15 ml/1 tbsp white wine vinegar

4 very fresh eggs

4 slices of Parma ham or smoked salmon

FOR THE ORANGE HOLLANDAISE:

30 ml/2 tbsp white wine vinegar

30 ml/2 tbsp white wine

Juice and grated zest of 1 orange

90 g/3$\frac{1}{2}$ oz/scant $\frac{1}{2}$ cup butter

2 egg yolks

Sea salt and freshly ground black pepper

Preheat the oven to 230°C/450°F/gas 8/fan oven 210°C. Snap off the woody ends of the asparagus and lay the spears on a baking (cookie) sheet. Brush them with oil and season lightly. Roast the spears for 5–10 minutes, depending on their thickness, until they just start to brown. Turn off the oven.

Put the toasted brioche on two plates, arrange the asparagus on top and put the plates in the oven, leaving the door ajar.

Bring a large frying pan full of water to a good rolling boil, add the vinegar and remove from the heat. Carefully break the eggs into the water and leave them for 10 minutes, by which time they will be perfectly poached.

Meanwhile, to make the Orange Hollandaise, put the vinegar, wine and orange juice in a small saucepan, bring to the boil and cook until syrupy and reduced to a spoonful – watch it as it will take no more than a couple of minutes.

Melt the butter gently in another small saucepan until it starts to bubble and 'sing'.

Whisk the egg yolks in a medium-sized bowl with an electric beater. Whisk in the orange zest, some pepper and the reduced juice/vinegar mixture, then slowly add the hot butter, a little at a time, continuing to whisk until it is thick and glossy. Check the seasoning as it may not need salt if the butter was salty.

By now the eggs should be ready, so take the plates out of the oven and arrange the Parma ham or smoked salmon on top of the asparagus. Remove the eggs from the water with a spatula, blot any excess water from the bottom of the spatula with a tea towel (dish cloth) or some kitchen paper (paper towels) and gently slide the eggs on to the ham or smoked salmon. Spoon the hollandaise over the eggs and serve immediately.

I love having lots of different flavours, colours and textures on my plate – every mouthful offers excitement and interest as I swap from one side of the plate to another, or work my way around it, enjoying each part of it in turn.

Combinations like the ones that follow also fill me with nostalgia: every taste is evocative and full of memories of holidays in the sunshine, of hillsides covered in wild herbs, of clamorous markets reeking of spices, of beachside restaurants with palm frond umbrellas…

All these recipes make a lovely lunch: when you are ready to eat, divide the three salads between two plates and serve with plenty of focaccia or ciabatta for the Italian plate, warm corn or flour tortillas for the Mexican plate, and pitta bread for the North African plate.

italian salad plate

sicilian peppers

1 large red (bell) pepper, about 200 g/7 oz

1 large yellow pepper, about 200 g/7 oz

15 g/¹/₂ oz raisins

15 g/¹/₂ oz/2 tbsp pine nuts

45 ml/3 tbsp olive oil

5 ml/1 tsp balsamic vinegar

1 garlic clove, peeled and crushed

Sea salt and freshly ground black pepper

30 ml/2 tbsp coarsely chopped fresh mint

Heat the grill (broiler) to high and grill (broil) the peppers 10 cm/4 in from the heat, turning as necessary, until their skins are black and blistered all over.

Meanwhile, place the raisins in a ramekin (custard cup) or small bowl and pour boiling water over them – this will plump them up and soften them.

Heat the oven to 160°C/325°F/gas 3/fan oven 145°C. Place the pine nuts on a baking (cookie) sheet and roast them for about 20 minutes until lightly golden. Remove from the oven and allow to cool.

When the peppers are ready, allow them to cool enough to handle. Peel, remove the stem and seeds and cut the flesh into 1 cm/¹/₂ in strips. Place in a bowl and add the oil, vinegar, garlic and some seasoning. (The peppers can be prepared up to this stage a day or two ahead and left to mellow in the fridge.)

Drain the raisins, squeeze them gently to get rid of any excess moisture, then stir them into the pepper mixture with the pine nuts and mint.

 Slightly sweet, slightly sharp, silky grilled peppers and crunchy pine nuts – this dish is full of Arab influences, like much of Sicilian cuisine.

borlotti bean purée

200 g/7 oz dried borlotti (pinto) beans

3 garlic cloves, peeled

1 bay leaf

Sea salt and freshly ground black pepper

90 ml/6 tbsp olive oil

Rinse the beans thoroughly, place them in a saucepan and cover with water. Add the garlic and bay leaf, bring to the boil, turn the heat right down, and simmer, covered, for about 2 hours until beautifully soft. Check them every now and then and, if they are looking a bit dry, add some more water but only enough to keep them covered.

Allow the beans to cool slightly. Using a slotted spoon, transfer them to a food processor, leaving most of the liquid behind. Add some seasoning and the oil and process until smooth – you may need to add some of the cooking liquid to make the blades turn.

The purée can be served hot or cold, and reheats nicely in a bowl over a pan of boiling water.

 Unlike haricot (navy), butter (lima) and red kidney beans, borlotti beans do not take well to canning. Their wonderfully creamy texture is lost and they acquire a faint but decidedly unpleasant metallic taste. I therefore always cook borlotti beans from scratch – they take only a couple of hours and simmer away happily without attention so only a very small amount of forward planning is required – and they give a wonderfully rich and deeply flavoured purée. If, however, you are pushed for time, you could use the haricot (navy) bean purée on page 34.

rocket and tomato salad

125 g/4½ oz cherry tomatoes, quartered

3 sun-dried tomatoes in olive oil, snipped into slivers with scissors

30 g/1¼ oz rocket leaves

25 g/1 oz red onion, peeled and thinly sliced

1 garlic clove, peeled and crushed

45 ml/3 tbsp oil from the sun-dried tomatoes

30 g/1¼ oz /scant ⅓ cup freshly grated Parmesan cheese

Sea salt and freshly ground black pepper

Mix together all the ingredients in a salad bowl just before serving.

 It is important to use freshly grated Parmesan cheese for this salad – the ready-grated stuff in a tub is too powdery. The grating discs that come with food processors are ideal as they give long thin strips of cheese that add texture. You could also use a vegetable peeler to make larger strips, but then the cheese will not be so well distributed or cling so deliciously to the rocket.

Bean and Sweetcorn Salad
Red kidney beans, *frijoles*, are the
most Mexican of foods – the
majority of the population
virtually lives on them. This salad
is very ample indeed for two
because it uses a whole can of
beans, but it keeps well so if you
do not finish it in one go (which is
extremely unlikely!) the leftovers
will still be wonderful the
following day. Do not be tempted
to use ground cumin – toasting
the seeds enhances their flavour
considerably, and their texture is
lovely.

Avocado Salad
Try not to make this salad too far
ahead as it does not keep well: the
avocado loses its colour and the
tomatoes go watery. Feel free to
add a finely chopped chilli if you
fancy a bit of extra heat.

Potatoes with Chorizo
These wonderfully gutsy and spicy
potatoes can be served hot or at
room temperature, but the chorizo
is definitely more aromatic when
hot.

mexican salad plate

bean and sweetcorn salad

5 ml/1 tsp cumin seeds

1 x 400 g/14 oz/large can of red kidney beans, rinsed and drained

100 g/4 oz frozen or tinned sweetcorn, thawed or rinsed and drained

30 g/1¼ oz red onion, peeled and finely chopped

1 garlic clove, peeled and crushed

1 hot green or red chilli, seeded and finely chopped

75 g/3 oz red (bell) pepper, seeded and diced

30 ml/2 tbsp olive oil

10 ml/ 2 tsp wine vinegar

Sea salt and freshly ground black pepper

75 g/3 oz/¾ cup Feta cheese, crumbled

30 ml/2 tbsp coarsely chopped fresh coriander (cilantro)

Toast the cumin seeds in a small heavy-based pan over a medium heat until
they are aromatic. Grind them coarsely in a mortar or spice grinder.

Place them in a salad bowl, add all the other ingredients except the cheese and
coriander, and stir well.

Fold in the cheese and coriander just before serving.

avocado salad

2 small, ripe avocados

100 g/4 oz cherry tomatoes, quartered

30 g/1¼ oz red onion, peeled and finely chopped

1 garlic clove, peeled and crushed

30 ml/2 tbsp olive oil

15 ml/1 tbsp lemon juice

Sea salt and freshly ground black pepper

Peel the avocados, place them in a bowl and mash them coarsely with a fork.

Carefully fold in all the remaining ingredients, seasoning to taste.

potatoes with chorizo

400 g/14 oz potatoes, cut into 2 cm/¾ in cubes

100 g/4 oz red onions, peeled and sliced

45 ml/3 tbsp olive oil

Sea salt and freshly ground black pepper

100 g/4 oz chorizo, diced

15 ml/1 tbsp chipotle chilli sauce (available from delicatessens or the speciality section of large supermarkets)

Preheat the oven to 200°C/400°F/gas 6/fan oven 180°C. Cook the potatoes in salted boiling water for 10 minutes. Drain well and place in a roasting tray. Stir in the onions, oil and plenty of seasoning. Roast for about 1 hour, stirring every 15 minutes, until crusty and golden.

Meanwhile, gently fry the chorizo in a dry frying pan, stirring occasionally, for about 10 minutes until it has rendered its fat. Scoop it out with a slotted spoon and leave it to drain on a plate lined with kitchen paper (paper towels).

When the potatoes are ready, stir in the chipotle and chorizo and serve at once or set aside to cool.

Aubergine Salad
A classic Moroccan salad that may not score highly on looks but certainly does on flavour! The aubergine is normally salted and left to drain before being fried, but I can never be bothered – and I always try to roast aubergine anyway because it absorbs so much oil when fried.

Orange Salad
A fresh, sharp, colourful salad that also makes an excellent first course. I have slotted it in with North African dishes because we often ate it in Tunisia, but I have come across variations of it in Greece and Sicily as well.

Moorish Spinach and Chick Peas
Sweet and sour combinations, like the raisins and yoghurt in this dish, are found throughout the Mediterranean and are one of the hallmarks of Moorish cuisine. This is equally good hot or cold.

north african salad plate

aubergine salad

500 g/18 oz aubergine (eggplant), cut into 1 cm/^{1}/$_2$ in chunks

Sea salt and freshly ground black pepper

75 ml/5 tbsp olive oil

5 ml/1 tsp cumin seeds

1.5 ml/^{1}/$_4$ tsp sweet paprika

2 garlic cloves, peeled and crushed

300 g/11 oz tomatoes, skinned and coarsely chopped

15 g/^{1}/$_2$ oz fresh coriander (cilantro), coarsely chopped

Preheat the oven to 200°C/400°F/gas 6/fan oven 180°C. Place the aubergine in a roasting tin, season and drizzle with 30 ml/2 tbsp of the oil. Roast, tossing occasionally, for about 1 hour until it is soft and golden.

Meanwhile, toast the cumin seeds in a small heavy-based pan until aromatic, then grind them coarsely in a mortar or spice grinder.

When the aubergine is ready, heat a heavy-based frying pan and scrape the aubergine into it. Add the cumin, paprika, garlic and some seasoning and fry gently for a couple of minutes, mashing the aubergines at the same time with a potato masher or the back of a wooden spoon.

Stir in the tomatoes, turn the heat right down and leave it all to simmer, stirring occasionally, until it is thick and dark. Allow to cool to room temperature, stir in the remaining oil and check the seasoning. Add the coriander just before serving.

 The salad can be served immediately or kept for 2 or 3 days in the fridge – it actually improves with keeping.

orange salad

2 large navel oranges

A handful of rocket leaves or watercress

20 g/³/₄ oz red onion, peeled and thinly sliced

6 black olives, stoned (pitted) and halved

50 g/2 oz/¹/₂ cup Feta cheese, crumbled

30 ml/2 tbsp olive oil

Sea salt and freshly ground black pepper (optional)

Peel the oranges with a sharp knife, removing all the pith, then slice them into rounds about 7.5 mm/¹/₃ in thick.

Place the rocket or watercress on a plate. Overlap the orange slices on top of it, sprinkle with the onion, olives and cheese and drizzle with oil. You can add some seasoning if you want, but I usually find it doesn't need it.

moorish spinach and chick peas

30 g/1¹/₄ oz raisins

20 g/³/₄ oz walnuts

200 g/7 oz baby spinach leaves, washed

1 x 400 g/14 oz/large can of chick peas (garbanzos), drained and rinsed

1 mild red chilli, seeded and chopped

100 ml/3¹/₂ fl oz/scant ¹/₂ cup Greek-style plain yoghurt

45 ml/3 tbsp olive oil

Sea salt and freshly ground black pepper

30 ml/2 tbsp chopped fresh mint

Preheat the oven to 160°C/325°F/gas 3/fan oven 145°C.

Place the raisins in a small bowl, cover them with boiling water and leave to soak for 30 minutes. Drain.

Place the walnuts on a baking (cookie) sheet and toast them in the oven for 15 minutes until lightly golden. Remove from the oven and allow to cool.

Heat a large saucepan or frying pan until really hot and throw in the spinach. Stir it around briskly until it is wilted and dark. Add the chick peas and continue stirring until they are hot.

Mix in the raisins, walnuts, chilli, yoghurt, oil and some seasoning. Sprinkle with the mint and either eat immediately or allow to cool to room temperature.

The vegetables in this recipe are cooked down until thick and 'jammy', which is presumably where the 'confiture' part comes in. We came across this confiture in Tunisia, where it was served cold and sprinkled with a strong salty cheese, as an accompaniment to grilled lamb chops – and very delicious it was too. The cheese is optional as it is just as good without.

A Tunisian cook would probably fry it all up from the start, but I prefer to roast the vegetables as this intensifies their flavour and makes the final dish lighter and less oily. The confiture has countless uses: it is really good with charcuterie, poached eggs, mixed into warm borlotti (pinto) beans … and so on.

grilled salmon with tunisian vegetable confiture

FOR THE CONFITURE:

500 g/18 oz tomatoes, halved

15 ml/1 tbsp runny honey

135 ml/4½ fl oz olive oil

Sea salt and freshly ground black pepper

500 g/18 oz aubergine (eggplant), cut into chunks

200 g/7 oz onions, peeled and coarsely chopped

2 garlic cloves, peeled and crushed

5 ml/1 tsp cumin seeds

5 ml/1 tsp sweet paprika

5 ml/1 tsp ground cinnamon

1 piece of Lemon Pickled in Salt and Lemon Juice (see page 19), finely chopped

50 g/2 oz/½ cup Feta cheese, crumbled

15 ml/1 tbsp chopped fresh mint

15 ml/1 tbsp chopped fresh coriander (cilantro)

FOR THE SALMON:

2 salmon fillets, about 200 g/7 oz each and 2 cm/¾ in thick

5 ml/1 tsp olive oil

Sea salt and freshly ground black pepper

Preheat the oven to 200°C/400°F/gas 6/fan oven 180°C.

To make the confiture, place the tomatoes, cut-sides up, on a baking (cookie) sheet lined with baking parchment. Drizzle first with the honey, then 15 ml/1 tbsp of the oil. Season well.

Place the aubergine chunks in a roasting tin, drizzle with 60 ml/4 tbsp of the oil and season well.

Place the tomatoes on the top shelf of the oven and the aubergine on the middle shelf. Roast for about 1 hour, stirring the aubergines once or twice, until they are soft and just starting to blacken along the edges.

While the tomatoes and aubergine are cooking, heat 30 ml/2 tbsp of the oil in a large frying pan, add the onion and garlic and cook, stirring every now and then, for about 20 minutes until soft and golden.

Toast the cumin seeds in a small saucepan over a gentle heat until they are aromatic, then tip them into a mortar and grind them coarsely; you can do this in an electric grinder if you prefer but make sure you do not end up with powder.

When the vegetables are ready, set the aubergine aside. Allow the tomatoes to cool slightly, then transfer to a food processor and process to medium-smooth.

When the onions are ready, stir in the cumin, paprika and cinnamon and cook for a couple of minutes. Add the aubergine and tomatoes, bring to the boil and simmer for 5 minutes. Stir in the pickled lemon and the remaining oil and check the seasoning.

Heat the grill (broiler) to high. Place the salmon on a foil-lined baking (cookie) sheet, brush with the oil, season and grill (broil) 10 cm/4 in from the heat for 5 minutes – test it with your thumb; it should still be slightly bouncy.

Place the salmon on two warm plates. Sprinkle the warm confiture with the cheese and herbs and serve immediately with the salmon.

 Do resist the temptation to skip toasting the cumin seeds and use ground cumin instead, because the heat really brings out their fragrance and flavour.

The raffish port of Trápani on the west coast of Sicily is famous for its fish stew, confusingly known as a *cuscus*. Each restaurant in the elegant Old Town seems to have its own little variation but, funnily enough, the best one we had was on the north coast, in Cefalù. Delicately scented with fennel, it was served with penne rather than couscous, which was a truly successful partnership as the sauce seeped into the pasta tubes and the texture was chewy and juicy.

cuscus alla trapanese

750 g/1³/₄ lb live mussels

30 ml/2 tbsp white wine

30 ml/2 tbsp olive oil

200 g/7 oz onions, peeled and coarsely chopped

2 garlic cloves, peeled and crushed

75 g/3 oz carrot, scrubbed and diced

125 g/4¹/₂ oz fennel bulb, coarsely chopped

3 cm/1¹/₄ in piece of cinnamon stick

5 ml/1 tsp fennel seeds, very coarsely ground

1 hot dried chilli, crumbled

1 x 400 g/14 oz/large can of chopped tomatoes

Sea salt and freshly ground black pepper

50 g/2 oz/¹/₂ cup freshly grated Parmesan cheese

10 raw king prawns (shrimp), shelled and deveined

250 g/9 oz tuna or swordfish, cut into strips

30 ml/2 tbsp chopped fresh parsley

TO SERVE:

Pasta or couscous

Scrub the mussels and remove the beards. Discard any that are broken.

Place the wine and mussels in a large saucepan and cook, covered, over a high heat for 2–3 minutes until they open. Set aside. When cool enough to handle, pick out four or six nice ones to use as garnish and remove the remainder from their shells. Keep the liquor to use in the sauce.

Heat the oil in a frying pan, add the onions and garlic and cook over a medium heat, stirring occasionally, for about 15 minutes until soft and golden.

Add the carrot and fennel, cover, turn the heat right down and leave to cook gently for 30 minutes.

Turn up the heat to medium again, stir in the cinnamon, fennel seeds and chilli and stir-fry for 1 minute. Add the to\matoes, the mussel liquor and some seasoning, and simmer, stirring occasionally for about 30 minutes until the sauce is nice and thick.

Stir in the cheese, prawns, tuna or swordfish and mussels and cook, stirring, just until the prawns turn pink.

Check the seasoning, sprinkle with the parsley and serve immediately over pasta or couscous.

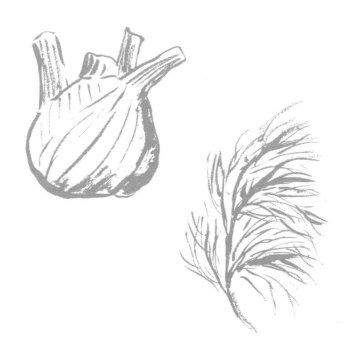

The smoked salmon makes these fish cakes rich and savoury, a perfect contrast to the fresh, vibrant salsa. We sometimes have them in a bun, like a hamburger.

They are also terrific picnic food, but if you are making them for this specific purpose, partner them with the Swedish apple and orange salad on page 70, as the Mexican Salsa will not travel well in a rucksack or hamper!

spicy salmon cakes with fruity mexican salsa

225 g/8 oz salmon fillet, skinned

30 ml/2 tbsp olive oil

75 g/3 oz red onions, peeled and coarsely chopped

1 garlic clove, peeled and crushed

1 hottish red or green chilli, seeded and finely chopped

10 ml/2 tsp Madras curry paste

175 g/6 oz cold mashed potato

2.5 ml/$\frac{1}{2}$ tsp sea salt

Juice and grated zest of 1 lemon

1 egg yolk

125 g/4$\frac{1}{2}$ oz smoked salmon, diced

65 g/2$\frac{1}{2}$ oz/1$\frac{1}{4}$ cups wholemeal breadcrumbs

FOR THE SALSA:

1 small mango, peeled and diced

10 g/scant $\frac{1}{2}$ oz red onion, peeled and finely chopped

1 garlic clove, peeled and chopped

1 red or green chilli, seeded and finely chopped

45 ml/3 tbsp olive oil

15 ml/1 tbsp lemon or lime juice

Sea salt and freshly ground black pepper

1 small avocado, peeled, stoned (pitted) and cut into 1 cm/$\frac{1}{2}$ in pieces

30 ml/2 tbsp chopped fresh coriander (cilantro)

Heat the grill (broiler) to high, place the fresh salmon on a foil-lined baking (cookie) sheet and grill (broil) 10 cm/4 in from the heat for 5 minutes if you are using a tail piece, 7–10 minutes for a thicker piece. Cool and then, using a fork, separate the flesh into large flakes.

Heat half the oil in a small saucepan, add the onions, garlic and chilli and cook over a medium heat, stirring occasionally, for about 10 minutes until soft and translucent. Stir in the curry paste and cook for a further 1 minute.

Place the mashed potato in a bowl, add the onion mixture, salt, lemon zest, 5 ml/1 tsp of the lemon juice and the egg yolk and mix well with a wooden spoon. Gently fold in the two salmons.

Divide the mixture into four and, using your hands, shape it into round cakes – a pastry (paste) ring makes this much easier! Put the breadcrumbs on a plate, drizzle the remaining olive oil over them and mix well with a fork. Carefully coat the salmon cakes with the breadcrumbs by placing them on the plate and patting the crumbs all over them. Transfer the cakes to a foil-lined baking (cookie) sheet and chill for at least 1 hour or overnight to firm up. Remove from the fridge 30 minutes before cooking.

To make the salsa, mix together all the ingredients except the avocado and coriander in a small bowl.

Preheat the oven to 200°C/400°F/gas 6/fan oven 180°C and bake the salmon cakes for 20 minutes.

Fold the avocado and coriander into the salsa, then serve immediately with the salmon cakes.

Tail pieces of salmon are ideal for this dish.

The salsa can be prepared 2 or 3 hours ahead of time.

The salmon cakes are also very good served cold.

Fish stews, called *suquets*, are served all along the French coasts. However, we came across a suquet in Barcelona, and discovered that it is a typical Catalán dish as well – hence the Catalán spelling of alioli – although in Catalunya it is thickened with a traditional spicy *picada* of nuts and breadcrumbs and laced with garlic mayonnaise. It is rich and unctuous, heady with garlic, incredibly savoury and satisfying.

The quantities in this recipe may seem excessive and it is certainly a meal in itself, serving two very nicely indeed, but you are very, very unlikely to have any left over!

I like to use part olive oil, part yoghurt in the garlic mayonnaise to lighten it and smooth out the flavour, which can be over-brutal.

suquet
with catalán alioli

FOR THE SUQUET:

30 ml/2 tbsp olive oil

200 g/7 oz onions, peeled and coarsely chopped

1 garlic clove, crushed

250 g/9 oz tomatoes, skinned and coarsely chopped

200 g/7 oz potatoes, peeled and cut into 1 cm/$^1/_2$ in dice

1 bay leaf

250 ml/8 fl oz/1 cup white wine

500 ml/17 fl oz/2$^1/_4$ cups chicken or fish stock

Sea salt and freshly ground black pepper

200 g/7 oz raw king prawns (shrimp), shelled and deveined

125 g/4$^1/_2$ oz salmon fillet, skinned and cut into 2 cm/$^3/_4$ in chunks

125 g/4$^1/_2$ oz cod fillet, skinned and cut into 2 cm/$^3/_4$ in chunks

30 ml/2 tbsp chopped fresh parsley

FOR THE PICADA:

25 g/1 oz/$^1/_4$ cup blanched almonds, toasted

10 g/scant $^1/_2$ oz wholemeal bread

1 garlic clove, peeled

5 ml/1 tsp pimentón (smoked paprika)

1.5 ml/$^1/_4$ tsp ground cinnamon

2.5 ml/$^1/_2$ tsp saffron strands

FOR THE CATALÁN ALIOLI:

2 egg yolks

2 garlic cloves, peeled and crushed

100 ml/3$^1/_2$ fl oz/scant $^1/_2$ cup olive oil

120 ml/4 fl oz/$^1/_2$ cup Greek-style plain yoghurt

Sea salt and freshly ground black pepper

Fresh lemon juice (optional)

To make the suquet, heat the oil in a large heavy-based saucepan and add the onions and garlic. Cook over a medium heat, stirring occasionally, for about 20 minutes until soft and golden.

Add the tomatoes and cook for a further 10 minutes.

Stir in the potatoes and bay leaf, then the wine, stock and some seasoning. Simmer, uncovered, for 20 minutes until the potato is cooked and the liquid reduced by a third. While the suquet is cooking, prepare the picada and then the alioli.

To make the picada, place all the ingredients in a food processor and process fairly finely. Set aside until needed.

To make the alioli, whisk the egg yolks and garlic in a small bowl with an electric whisk until slightly thickened, then slowly pour in the oil, whisking all the time until it is thick, pale and glossy. Whisk in the yoghurt and some seasoning. Taste and squeeze in some lemon juice if it is not sharp enough – it will depend on the acidity of the yoghurt.

Stir the picada into the suquet and simmer for a minute or two, then add the prawns and fish. Cook gently for a couple of minutes until they are just firm.

Remove from the heat, stir in 30 ml/2 tbsp of the alioli and the parsley, check the seasoning and serve immediately in big, deep soup bowls with a large dollop of the alioli on top. Add more alioli as you eat.

 The alioli can be prepared the day before and chilled, but it does tend to get stronger and more garlicky as it sits!

chicken with apricot, raisin and pickled lemon chutney

FOR THE CHUTNEY:

20 g/³/₄ oz raisins

40 g/1³/₄ oz dried apricots, diced

40 g/1³/₄ oz red onion, peeled and coarsely chopped

120 ml/4 fl oz/¹/₂ cup white wine

1 piece of Lemon Pickled in Salt and Lemon Juice (see page 19), finely chopped

30 ml/2 tbsp olive oil

5 ml/1 tsp balsamic vinegar

FOR THE CHICKEN:

6 chicken thighs

1.5 ml/¹/₄ tsp chilli powder

15 ml/1 tbsp finely chopped fresh rosemary

60 ml/4 tbsp olive oil

Sea salt and freshly ground black pepper

FOR THE YOGHURT:

120 ml/4 fl oz/¹/₂ cup Greek-style plain yoghurt

15 ml/1 tbsp olive oil

1 garlic clove, peeled and crushed

Sea salt and freshly ground black pepper

Start off with the chutney as it will need to cool. Place the raisins, apricots, onion and wine in a small saucepan and bring to the boil. Turn the heat right down and simmer gently, stirring occasionally, for about 15 minutes until most of the wine has been absorbed. Allow to cool to lukewarm, then stir in the pickled lemon, oil and vinegar.

The tartness of the Greek yoghurt creates a lovely contrast in this dish against the sweetness of the fruit and the salty pickle of the lemons. I often cook a couple of extra chicken thighs and make a double quantity of the chutney so we can fill some crusty ciabatta rolls with cold chicken and chutney for lunch the following day.

Place the chicken thighs in a small roasting tin. Stir together the chilli powder, rosemary, oil and some seasoning in a ramekin (custard cup), then rub it all over the chicken. If you have time, leave the chicken to marinate for an hour or two.

To make the yoghurt, mix together all the ingredients in a small bowl, seasoning to taste.

Preheat the oven to 200°C/400°F/gas 6/fan oven 180°C. Cook the chicken thighs for 30 minutes, basting every now and then with the juices.

Cover the chicken loosely with a piece of foil and allow to rest for 10 minutes before serving with the chutney and yoghurt.

 The chutney keeps well for several days in the refrigerator.

Very thin asparagus, known as sprue, works well in this recipe and has the bonus of being considerably cheaper. The sauce is also delicious with grilled (broiled) wild salmon and with a bowl of pasta and asparagus tips.

The flavours – and colours – in this dish are delicate so don't be tempted to make it outside the local asparagus season: if you use imported asparagus, the magic will vanish into thin air as your sauce will be a pretty green but taste of nothing.

chicken supremes with asparagus and parma ham

FOR THE SAUCE:

250 g/9 oz asparagus – this can be trimmings or pieces left over from the stuffing

100 ml/3¹/₂ fl oz/scant ¹/₂ cup double (heavy) cream

Sea salt and freshly ground black pepper

FOR THE CHICKEN SUPREMES:

24 to 32 slender asparagus spears, trimmed to about 10 cm/4 in long

2 chicken supremes, about 175 g/6 oz each

6 slices of Parma ham

15 g/¹/₂ oz/1 tbsp butter

Sea salt and freshly ground black pepper

To make the sauce, steam the asparagus for 15 minutes until soft. Place in the bowl of a food processor, add the cream and some seasoning and process until smooth. If you have a mouli-légumes, strain the sauce through the medium disc, otherwise push the sauce through a coarse sieve (strainer). This step is essential for a silky sauce, so don't be tempted to skip it!

To make the chicken supremes, steam the asparagus over a high heat for about 5 minutes until just tender. Set aside to cool.

Cut two pieces of foil, about 30 cm/12 in square. Place the chicken supremes between two pieces of clingfilm (plastic wrap) and bash them with a rolling pin to flatten them. Remove them from the clingfilm and place them on the foil, at the end nearest to you. Lay three slices of Parma ham on each chicken supreme and top with 6 to 8 asparagus spears, depending on their size. Fold the edges of the chicken suprêmes up and over the filling to enclose it and then, with the help of the foil, roll it all tightly into a sausage shape, twisting the ends of the foil like a Christmas cracker.

Lay the remaining asparagus spears, to be used as a garnish, in a small ovenproof dish, dot with the butter and sprinkle with salt and pepper.

Preheat the oven to 200°C/400°F/gas 6/fan oven 180°C. Place the chicken on a baking (cookie) sheet and cook for 25–30 minutes – the parcels should be firm to the touch. Set it aside to rest for 10 minutes.

Carefully reheat the sauce over gentle heat – and under no circumstances let it boil.

Just before you carve the chicken, place the asparagus garnish in the oven to heat. Remove the foil from the chicken and slice it into discs about 7.5 mm/ $^1/_3$ in thick. Arrange the slices in a semi-circle on warm plates, place some sauce in the middle, garnish with the asparagus spears and serve immediately.

The sauce can be prepared 2–3 hours in advance and then reheated very, very gently without boiling. It is not worth making it the day before as it would lose too much of its flavour.

The chicken can be prepared up to being wrapped in the foil up to 3 hours in advance and chilled, but remember to take it out of the fridge half an hour before you are ready to cook it.

The chicken takes on a welcome boldness from its well-flavoured Mediterranean partners – I know the salami sounds a bit weird but it makes a real contribution. Use a large, wide spatula to transfer the chicken from the baking dish to the plates and be sure to scrape up any bits of cheese that might have oozed out during the cooking.

The sauce can be prepared up to 24 hours in advance and chilled – but be warned that the longer it sits, the stronger it grows!

chicken with salami, goats' cheese and pimentón stuffing

1 large red (bell) pepper, about 200 g/7 oz

1 large yellow pepper, about 200 g/7 oz

2 chicken supremes

4 slices of salami

50 g/2 oz goats' cheese

Sea salt and freshly ground black pepper

FOR THE SAUCE:

120 ml/4 fl oz/$\frac{1}{2}$ cup Greek-style plain yoghurt

1 garlic clove, peeled and crushed

1.5 ml/$\frac{1}{4}$ tsp English mustard

2.5 ml/$\frac{1}{2}$ tsp pimentón (smoked paprika)

30 ml/2 tbsp olive oil

Sea salt and freshly ground black pepper

Heat the grill (broiler) to high and grill (broil) the peppers 10 cm/4 in from the heat until black and blistered all over. Allow to cool, then peel and remove the stem and seeds. Slice the flesh into long strips about 1 cm/$\frac{1}{2}$ in wide and set aside 4 strips of each colour for the stuffing.

To make the sauce, place the remaining pepper strips in a food processor with the yoghurt, garlic, mustard, pimentón, oil and some seasoning and process until smooth.

Preheat the oven to 200°C/400°F/gas 6/fan oven 180°C. Lay the supremes on a chopping board, fillet-side up. Open up the fillet like a book and, with a small knife, carefully slice along the flesh near the fillet to open the supreme out further.

Place the salami, 2 red pepper strips, 2 yellow pepper strips and half the cheese on each supreme and fold the flap back up and over the stuffing. Gently gather them up and place them, stuffing-side down, in an ovenproof dish. Tuck the ends in, season well and bake in the oven for 20 minutes until firm to the touch. Turn off the oven, leave the door ajar and leave the chicken to rest for 10 minutes.

Transfer the chicken to two warm plates with a spatula, pour any cooking juices over it, and serve with the sauce.

Quail are impossible to eat daintily or elegantly, unless you are prepared to go hungry! A knife and fork will provide you with a small quantity of flavoursome, very faintly gamey meat but if you want to make a proper meal of them, relax and use your fingers to chew the flesh off the bones.

Salsa Romesco is a bold and brassy sauce from Catalunya, slightly spicy from smoked paprika, rich with roasted peppers and nuts, and thickened with breadcrumbs. I love it with everything from stir-fried prawns to poached eggs on toast or freshly cooked pasta. Although the list of ingredients for this dish looks long, it is simple to prepare.

roast quail with vegetable gratin and salsa romesco

FOR THE SALSA:

1 large red (bell) pepper, about 200 g/7 oz

1 garlic clove, peeled

30 g/1¼ oz skinned, toasted hazelnuts (filberts)

2.5 ml/½ tsp pimentón (smoked paprika)

30 g/1¼ oz wholemeal bread, roughly torn into pieces

250 ml/8 fl oz/1 cup olive oil

15 ml/1 tbsp red wine or sherry vinegar

Sea salt and freshly ground black pepper

FOR THE GRATIN:

1 large aubergine (eggplant), about 350 g/12 oz, cut into large chunks

200 g/7 oz courgettes (zucchini), cut into large chunks

350 g/12 oz sweet potatoes, peeled and cut into large chunks

Sea salt and freshly ground black pepper

2.5 ml/½ tsp ground cinnamon

90 ml/6 tbsp olive oil

100 g/4 oz/2 cups soft wholemeal breadcrumbs

50 g/2 oz/½ cup freshly grated Parmesan cheese

100 g/4 oz Feta cheese

FOR THE QUAIL:

4 quail

10 ml/2 tsp runny honey

Sea salt and freshly ground black pepper

15 ml/1 tbsp chopped fresh rosemary

To make the salsa, heat the grill (broiler) to high and grill (broil) the pepper until blistered and black all over. Set aside until cool enough to handle, then peel and discard the seeds and stalk.

Place in a food processor with the garlic, hazelnuts, pimentón and bread and process until smooth. With the motor still running, slowly pour in the oil and vinegar and add some seasoning.

To make the gratin, preheat the oven to 200°C/400°F/gas 6/fan oven 180°C. Place the vegetables in a gratin dish, season well, sprinkle with the cinnamon and drizzle with 60 ml/4 tbsp of the oil. Roast for about 45 minutes, stirring occasionally, until soft and starting to brown.

Smear the honey over the quails, season and sprinkle with the rosemary.

Mix together the breadcrumbs, Parmesan cheese and remaining oil in a small bowl.

When the vegetables are ready, crumble the Feta over them, spoon the breadcrumb mixture evenly over everything and nestle the quails down comfortably into the gratin, breast-side up. Return to the oven and cook for 10 minutes. Turn off the oven, leave the door open and allow to rest for 10 minutes before serving with the salsa.

 The salsa can be prepared well ahead of time and will keep in the fridge for 24 hours.

Another utterly simple dish raised to dizzy heights by a gutsy tapenade, which perfumes the flesh and mingles deliciously with the roasting juices; and the aroma emanating from the oven while it cooks will draw cats, dogs and hungry humans to your kitchen door!

roast chicken with roasted tomato tapenade

1 x 1 kg/2¹/₄ lb chicken

1 quantity of Roasted Fresh Tomato Tapenade (see page 118)

About 15 ml/1 tbsp olive oil

Sea salt and freshly ground black pepper

Preheat the oven to 200°C/400°F/gas 6/fan oven 180°C.

Gently and carefully loosen the skin on the chicken breast and as far down over the drumsticks and thighs as you can go. You can do this with your fingers (but beware of long fingernails which can tear the skin!) or with the handle of a wooden spoon, which I find easier. Insert spoonfuls of tapenade under the skin, again pushing it in as far as you can. Then massage the skin on the outside to distribute the tapenade well. Rub some oil into the skin and season well.

Roast the chicken, breast-side up, for 45 minutes. Allow it to rest for 10 minutes before carving.

Serve with the cooking juices and any leftover tapenade.

Spain has a strong and ancient hunting tradition, and the Alpujarra Mountains to the east of Granada are teeming with game in the autumn. We had this wonderful pheasant casserole there during a walking holiday several years ago and this is my version. The raisins point to a Moorish origin, while chorizo is a local speciality, one of the many *embutidos* (charcuterie) for which the Alpujarras are renowned.

Cock pheasants are tougher than hens but have more flavour and are better for stewing.

The cooking time can vary depending on the age of the pheasant, so test the pheasant for tenderness with a fork and, if you encounter resistance, cook if for a further 20 minutes.

faisán del andaluz

30 ml/2 tbsp olive oil

1 cock pheasant, jointed

100 g/4 oz chorizo, sliced into 1 cm/¹/₂ in rounds

100 g/4 oz onions, peeled and sliced

1 large red (bell) pepper, about 200 g/7 oz, seeded and cut into 1 cm/¹/₂ in strips

1 large orange pepper, about 200 g/7 oz, seeded and cut into 1 cm/¹/₂ cm strips

2 garlic cloves, peeled and crushed

1 heaped tsp pimentón (smoked paprika)

250 ml/8 fl oz/1 cup white wine

1 heaped tsp bouillon powder

1 bay leaf

A large sprig of rosemary

Sea salt and freshly ground black pepper

25 g/1 oz black olives, stoned (pitted)

25 g/1 oz raisins

15 ml/1 tbsp snipped fresh chives

Heat half the oil in a heavy-based frying pan and brown the pheasant pieces on all sides. Transfer to a plate and set aside.

Add the chorizo to the frying pan and cook until golden. Using a slotted spoon, transfer the rounds to a plate lined with kitchen paper (paper towels). Discard the chorizo fat and wipe out the frying pan.

Return the frying pan to the heat, add the remaining oil and the onions, peppers and garlic. Cook over a medium heat, stirring occasionally, until soft and starting to colour.

Sprinkle in the pimentón and cook for 1 minute longer, then pour in the wine. Bring to the boil, add the bouillon powder, the herbs and some seasoning and stir well. Arrange the pheasant pieces, skin-side up, on top of the vegetables, cover and cook over a low heat for 40 minutes.

Stir in the chorizo, olives and raisins and cook for a further 20 minutes until the pheasant is tender and the sauce thick and aromatic. Sprinkle with the chives and serve.

wood pigeon with figs and oranges

1 large orange

15 ml/1 tbsp olive oil

2 wood pigeons

30 ml/2 tbsp Cointreau or Grand Marnier

250 ml/8 fl oz/1 cup red wine

Sea salt and freshly ground black pepper

2 fresh figs

Lemon juice (optional)

Finely grate the zest from the orange and set aside. Peel the orange with a sharp knife and cut out the segments, reserving any juice.

Preheat the oven to 200°C/400°F/gas 6/fan oven 180°C. Heat the oil in a casserole (Dutch oven) large enough to hold the pigeons with a bit of room to spare. Brown the pigeons well on all sides, then sit them on their backs. Stand well back and pour the Cointreau or Grand Marnier over them. When the hissing and spluttering has subsided, add the wine and some seasoning and bring to the boil. Cover the casserole, place it in the oven and cook for 45 minutes.

Nestle the two figs into the sauce beside the pigeons and return the casserole to the oven for a further 15 minutes.

Turn off the oven. Carefully lift the pigeons and the figs out of the casserole, put them on a plate and return them to the oven, leaving the door ajar, to rest and keep warm while you deal with the sauce.

Add the reserved orange juice and grated zest to the sauce and boil it over a high heat until it is thick and syrupy – this will take only 5–10 minutes.

Add the orange segments and swirl them around just long enough to heat them through. Check the seasoning and add some lemon juice if the sauce is a bit sweet (it will depends on the sweetness of the orange).

Place the pigeons and figs on two warm plates, pour the sauce over them and serve immediately.

Wherever you go in Spain, paella is on the menu in virtually every restaurant – and it is always for a minimum of two people, which is incredibly frustrating because the SNP is happy to eat paella once during a holiday but never twice, and I adore it. However, I am free to cook it at home whenever I want and my simplified version, in which I add the cooked rice to the other ingredients, may be far from authentic but it is fuss-free and delicious.

paella valenciana para dos

1.5 ml/¼ tsp ground turmeric

1 chicken, vegetable or fish stock cube

125 g/4½ oz/generous ½ cup brown basmati rice

125 g/4½ oz chorizo, sliced into 1 cm/½ in rounds

2 chicken thighs

60 ml/4 tbsp olive oil

2 garlic cloves, peeled and crushed

300 g/11 oz onions, peeled and coarsely chopped

1 large red (bell) pepper, about 200 g/7 oz, seeded and cut into 2 cm/¾ in strips

120 ml/4 fl oz/½ cup white wine

2.5 ml/½ tsp saffron strands

200 g/7 oz raw king prawns (shrimp), shelled and deveined

Sea salt and freshly ground black pepper

30 ml/2 tbsp chopped fresh parsley

Bring a pan of salted water to the boil, add the turmeric, stock cube and rice, cover and cook on a low heat for 50 minutes.

Meanwhile, fry the chorizo in a small dry frying pan until golden on both sides. Using a slotted spoon, transfer it to a plate lined with kitchen paper (paper towels) and leave to drain.

Add the chicken thighs to the pan and brown them well on both sides. Set aside.

Heat the oil in a large frying pan, add the garlic and onions and cook over a medium heat, stirring occasionally, for about 15 minutes until soft but not browned. Add the pepper strips and cook for a further 10 minutes.

Pour in the wine and let it bubble briefly, then add the chicken, cover the pan, turn down the heat to low and simmer for 30 minutes.

Just before the rice is ready, add the saffron, chorizo, prawns and some seasoning to the chicken mixture and stir-fry until the prawns just turn pink. Stir in the drained rice and turn the whole mixture over and over again with a large spoon to mix it well and allow the rice to absorb the flavours.

Sprinkle with the parsley and serve immediately.

A long, slow, gentle cooking produces meltingly tender meat and a richly flavoured, aromatic, faintly sweet sauce. Mashed potatoes are the perfect accompaniment. Get your butcher to remove the skin from the pork as it can be a bit of a struggle to do this yourself at home and if you leave it on it will cook to a rubbery toughness.

braised belly of pork with apple and cider

750 g/1³/₄ lb belly of pork, skin removed, bones left in

200 g/7 oz onions, peeled and coarsely chopped

3 bushy sprigs of rosemary

Sea salt and freshly ground black pepper

500 ml/17 fl oz/2¹/₄ cups dry cider

1 eating (dessert) apple, about 175 g/6 oz, peeled, cored and cut into 1 cm/¹/₂ in pieces

1 x 400 g/14 oz/large can of butter (lima) beans, drained and rinsed

Heat a casserole (Dutch oven) large enough to hold the pork over a medium heat and place the pork in it, fat-side down. Cook it, shifting it around every now and then with a spatula, until it is a nice deep gold – it needs to have some colour or your sauce will be pale and uninteresting. Transfer the pork to a plate and set aside. Preheat the oven to 180°C/350°F/gas 4/fan oven 160°C.

Add the onions to the pan and fry gently, stirring occasionally, for about 20 minutes until soft and golden.

Add the rosemary and some seasoning to the casserole and place the pork and any cooking juices on top. Pour in the cider, cover the pan and cook in the oven for 1¹/₂ hours.

Give it all a good stir round, then add the apple and beans, pushing them down into the sauce. Return the casserole to the oven for a further 30 minutes.

Transfer the pork to a warm plate, cover it with foil and leave to rest for 15 minutes. If the sauce looks a bit thin, simmer it down while the pork rests, and check the seasoning.

To serve, you can either just pull the meat from the bones – it will come away quite easily with a knife and fork – or slice down between the bones somewhere near the middle and cut it into two hunks.

I have read somewhere that kleftiko is known as 'The Dish of Thieves' or 'Bandit's Lamb' but I have no idea why – perhaps because, depending on the cut you use, it can be left to cook unattended for as long as it takes to steal a sheep!

Kleftiko is normally cooked in a paper parcel – as in 'en papillote' – but a snug china baking dish well wrapped in foil makes it all much less fiddly.

lamb kleftiko with red onion and feta

2 large lamb leg steaks, about 250 g/9 oz each

75 ml/5 tbsp olive oil

Sea salt and freshly ground black pepper

2 bay leaves

15 ml/1 tbsp fresh oregano leaves

4 garlic cloves, peeled and chopped

30 g/1¼ oz red onion, peeled and thinly sliced

100 g/4 oz tomatoes, skinned and thickly sliced

100 g/4 oz Feta cheese

Preheat the oven to 200°C/400°F/gas 6/fan oven 180°C.

Trim any excess fat off the steaks. Heat 15 ml/1 tbsp of the oil in a heavy-based frying pan until it is really hot and brown the steaks on both sides until they are well coloured (this is important for the flavour of the dish).

Place the steaks in a small baking dish – they need to fit quite snugly – and season them well. Arrange the herbs, garlic, onion and tomato slices on top and season again, then drizzle with the remaining oil and crumble the Feta over it all. Wrap the dish tightly in two layers of kitchen foil and bake in the oven for 1½ hours.

Heat the grill (broiler) to high. Unwrap the dish and place it under the grill, about 10 cm/4 in from the heat, for 5 minutes to brown the top. Serve immediately.

A number of years ago, during a winter holiday in Cyprus, we stopped for lunch at a tiny family-run taverna high up in the Troodos mountains. It was a cold, grey, damp day and the roaring fire in the dining-room was so welcoming I almost cried. And the smell of the lamb skewers grilling over small branches of oregano... I have never been able to reproduce their haunting, charred herbiness, as my oregano plant has never managed to grow strong and healthy enough to produce branches in our cool, lacklustre climate!

Chimichurri is a parsley vinaigrette from Argentinian cuisine and I have expanded the basic concept by adding Greek-style ingredients to go with my Cypriot lamb. You can use fillet of lamb if you prefer – more tender but much more expensive and the flavour is not quite in the same league.

garlic and oregano marinated lamb skewers

350 g/12 oz lamb leg steaks, trimmed and cut into 2 cm/³/₄ in cubes

30 ml/2 tbsp fresh oregano leaves

1 large garlic clove, peeled and crushed

30 ml/2 tbsp olive oil

1 small red onion, about 100 g/4 oz, peeled and quartered

FOR THE CHIMICHURRI:

25 g/1 oz fresh flatleaf parsley

30 ml/2 tbsp fresh oregano leaves

1 garlic clove, peeled

1 hot red chilli, seeded

120 ml/4 fl oz/¹/₂ cup olive oil

15 ml/1 tbsp lemon juice

Sea salt and freshly ground black pepper

50 g/2 oz/¹/₂ cup Feta cheese, crumbled

25 g/1 oz red onion, peeled and finely chopped (use any onion bits left over from the skewers)

TO SERVE:

Pitta bread

Tie up the lamb, oregano, garlic and oil in a freezer bag and leave it to marinate, shaking it occasionally, for about 1 hour.

Separate the quartered onion into layers, keeping the smaller ones for the chimichurri. Remove the lamb cubes from the marinade and thread them on to flat metal skewers, interspersing them here and there with a piece of onion. Lay the skewers in a foil-lined roasting tin and pour any remaining marinade from the bag over them.

Heat the grill (broiler) to high, place the roasting tin about 10 cm/4 in from the heat, and grill (broil) the skewers for 10 minutes, turning them over half-way through.

Meanwhile, to make the chimichurri, place the herbs, garlic, chilli, oil, lemon juice and some seasoning in a food processor. Process until fairly smooth and scrape into a small bowl. Stir in the Feta and onion.

Serve the lamb skewers with the chimichurri and pitta bread.

 If it is convenient, the chimichurri can be made a couple of hours ahead of time – but any longer and it starts to lose its vivid colour.

Fabadas – bean stews – are found all over Spain, the most famous being the rich and utterly piggy Fabada Asturiana, which boasts a variety of different sausages. The fabada we ate in Barcelona was somewhat lighter and included longaniza (a Catalán chorizo) and black and white butifarras (Catalán blood sausages). Lacking both, I tried making my fabada with ordinary Spanish chorizo and black pudding. The result was this deeply flavoured and aromatic stew.

If you want to be really authentic, don't discard the chorizo fat but use it to cook the vegetables – but your heart may protest!

roast rack of lamb with fabada catalana

FOR THE FABADA:

50 g/2 oz Spanish chorizo, diced

30 ml/2 tbsp olive oil

125 g/4$^{1}/_{2}$ oz onions, peeled and roughly chopped

100 g/4 oz leek, white part only, washed and sliced

90 g/3$^{1}/_{2}$ oz carrots, scrubbed and diced

2 garlic cloves, peeled and crushed

2 streaky bacon rashers (slices), rinded and chopped

1 bay leaf

A sprig of fresh rosemary

Sea salt and freshly ground black pepper

15 ml/1 tbsp brandy

250 ml/8 fl oz/1 cup red wine

250 ml/8 fl oz/1 cup vegetable or chicken stock – bouillon powder is fine

1 x 400 g/14 oz/large can of haricot (navy) beans, drained and rinsed

50 g/2 oz black pudding (blood sausage), cut into 1 cm/$^{1}/_{2}$ in thick slices

FOR THE LAMB:

2.5 ml/$^{1}/_{2}$ tsp runny honey

1 rack of lamb, fat removed

30 ml/2 tbsp finely chopped fresh rosemary

To make the fabada, heat a medium-sized heavy-bottomed saucepan or frying pan, add the chorizo and cook over a gentle heat for about 10 minutes until it has released most of its fat. Using a slotted spoon, transfer the chorizo to a plate lined with kitchen paper (paper towels). Discard the fat and wipe out the pan.

Return the pan to the heat and add the oil. Stir in the onions, leek, carrots, garlic, bacon, herbs and some seasoning and cook over a medium heat, stirring occasionally, for about 15 minutes until everything has softened and is starting to brown.

Pour in the brandy and let it bubble for a few seconds, then add the wine and stock. Bring to the boil, add the beans and black pudding, turn the heat to low and cook gently for 20 minutes until thick and well reduced.

While the fabada is cooking, preheat the oven to 200°C/400°F/gas 6/fan oven 180°C. Smear the honey over the lamb and sprinkle with the rosemary. Roast for 15 minutes. Turn off the oven and leave the meat inside to rest for 10 minutes with the door ajar.

Carve into 6 cutlets and serve on top of the fabada.

Don't be put off by this korma's unattractive appearance! The sauce is sludge-coloured and curdled-looking, but the flavour more than makes up for these shortcomings.

Kormas tend to be soothing dishes, gently spiced and mellow with cream or yoghurt, which I like to pep up with a bit of background warmth from hot chillies, but, if you are not a fire-eater, do use mild, red chillies instead.

mellow beef korma with yoghurt

4 whole cloves

10 ml/2 tsp coriander (cilantro) seeds

6 green cardamom pods

350 g/12 oz onions, peeled and coarsely chopped

5 garlic cloves, peeled

50 g/2 oz fresh root ginger, peeled and coarsely chopped

1 hot red chilli, halved and seeded

1 hot green chilli, halved and seeded

30 ml/2 tbsp olive oil

300 g/11 oz chuck steak, cut into 2 cm/³/₄ in pieces

120 ml/4 fl oz/¹/₂ cup Greek-style plain yoghurt

Sea salt and freshly ground black pepper

350 ml/12 fl oz/1¹/₃ cups chicken or vegetable stock – bouillon powder will do

15 g/¹/₂ oz fresh coriander (cilantro), coarsely chopped

TO SERVE:

Rice or Indian breads

Grind the cloves, coriander seeds and cardamom pods in an electric spice grinder.

Place the onions, garlic, ginger and chillies in a food processor and process to a coarse purée.

Heat the oil in a heavy saucepan. Add the steak and cook over a medium heat, stirring often, until the meat is well browned.

When the beef is ready, add the spice mix and stir-fry for 1 minute, then add the onion mixture and cook, stirring occasionally, until thick and golden.

Stir in the yoghurt and some seasoning and cook for a further 10 minutes or so, by which time the meat will have absorbed the yoghurt. Pour in the stock and bring to the boil. Turn the heat right down, cover and simmer very gently for 1 hour.

Remove the lid and, if the sauce looks a bit runny, turn up the heat and let it bubble energetically, uncovered, until the sauce coats the meat nicely.

Check the seasoning, sprinkle with the coriander and serve immediately with plenty of rice, naan bread or parathas to soak up the delectable sauce.

There is no particularly distinct flavour of coconut in this dish, but the result is a deeply flavoured and aromatic sauce with definite Eastern connotations.

Coconut features extensively in the cooking of Goa, softening the edges of its liberal use of chillies – and if you fancy increasing the heat, do not hesitate to add a couple of extra chillies to this Goan lamb.

spiced goan lamb in coconut milk

300 g/11 oz onions, peeled and coarsely chopped

2 garlic cloves, peeled

3 cm/1^1/$_4$ in piece of fresh root ginger, peeled and coarsely chopped

45 ml/3 tbsp olive oil

400 g/14 oz stewing lamb, cut into 2 cm/^{3}/$_4$ in pieces

10 green cardamom pods

1 hot green chilli, halved and seeded

1 hot red chilli, halved and seeded

10 ml/2 tsp ground cinnamon

1.5 ml/^{1}/$_4$ tsp ground cloves

2.5 ml/^{1}/$_2$ tsp ground turmeric

Sea salt and freshly ground black pepper

1 x 400 g/14 oz/large can of coconut milk

25 g/1 oz creamed coconut

10 g/scant ^{1}/$_2$ oz fresh coriander (cilantro), coarsely chopped

100 g/4 oz/1 cup roasted cashew nuts, coarsely chopped

Place the onions, garlic and ginger in the bowl of a food processor and process until finely chopped.

Heat the oil in a saucepan over a low heat, add the onion mixture and cook it, stirring occasionally, until the moisture has evaporated. Raise the heat to medium, add the lamb and stir-fry until it is well browned.

Grind the cardamoms very coarsely in a spice grinder or a mortar – just enough to bruise them and loosen the seeds. Stir them into the lamb along with the chillies, the other spices and some seasoning, and cook it all together for a minute or two.

Pour in the coconut milk, turn the heat down to low, cover the saucepan and let the lamb simmer away gently for at least 1 hour, preferably 2. Check it every now and then to ensure it is not drying out and add a little water if necessary.

Add the creamed coconut cream, stirring to melt it. Check the seasoning, sprinkle with the coriander and cashews and serve.

Root vegetables tend to have a slight sweetness, which is intensified by roasting and goes incredibly well with the coconuttiness of the pesto – but feel free to substitute any other vegetables that you fancy.

The vegetables make a nice lunch or supper dish on their own, or with Indian breads such as naan or parathas; but if you want to make it more substantial, try stirring a couple of cans of well-drained chick peas (garbanzos) or butter beans (lima beans) into the vegetables five minutes before the end of their cooking time.

roasted root vegetables with coriander, cashew and coconut

250 g/9 oz sweet potato, peeled and cut into 3 cm/1¼ in chunks

250 g/9 oz parsnip, peeled and cut into 3 cm/1¼ in chunks

250 g/9 oz celeriac (celery root), peeled and cut into 3 cm/1¼ in chunks

250 g/9 oz swede (rutabaga), peeled and cut into 3 cm/1¼ in chunks

2 bay leaves

2 sprigs of fresh rosemary

75 ml/5 tbsp toasted sesame oil

Sea salt and freshly ground black pepper

1 quantity of Coriander, Cashew and Coconut Pesto (see page 17)

Preheat the oven to 200°C/400°F/gas 6/fan oven 180°C.

Place the vegetables and herbs in a large roasting tin, drizzle them with the oil and season well. Roast for about 1 hour, stirring occasionally, until they are soft and starting to blacken around the edges.

Serve immediately with the pesto.

mediterranean scalloped potatoes

own with a salad, or with poached eggs, a steak or grilled salmon. And in the unlikely event that you have any left over, they are incredibly good cold for lunch the following day.

500 g/18 oz potatoes, scrubbed and cut into 5 mm/¹/₄ in thick slices

Sea salt and freshly ground black pepper

125 g/4¹/₂ oz red onions, peeled and sliced

2 garlic cloves, peeled and sliced

10 black olives, stoned (pitted) and halved

30 ml/2 tbsp fresh thyme leaves

250 g/9 oz tomatoes, cut into 5 mm/¹/₄ in thick slices

100 ml/3¹/₂ fl oz/scant ¹/₂ cup dry white wine

100 ml/3¹/₂ fl oz/scant ¹/₂ cup olive oil

50 g/2 oz/1 cup wholemeal breadcrumbs

50 g/2 oz/¹/₂ cup freshly grated Parmesan cheese

Preheat the oven to 200°C/400°F/gas 6/fan oven 180°C.

Cook the potatoes in salted boiling water for 5 minutes, drain well and place in a gratin dish. Season and stir around a bit to distribute the seasoning. Cover with the onion and garlic, then the olives and thyme and finally the tomatoes, seasoning as you go. Pour the wine and oil over the whole dish.

Mix together the breadcrumbs and cheese, then sprinkle over the potatoes.

Roast in the oven for 1 hour until the breadcrumbs are golden and the juices bubbling around the sides.

gigantes – cretan oven-baked

I couldn't believe the size of the butter beans in Crete – almost on a par with my thumb! Traditionally, gigantes (Greek for butter beans) are baked in the oven for hours until their wonderfully creamy texture has absorbed all the flavour and richness of the sauce they are cooked in, as well as the faintest whiff of wood smoke if the oven is wood-fired – which it often is in the mountain villages.

45 ml/3 tbsp olive oil

300 g/11 oz onions, peeled and roughly chopped

3 garlic cloves, peeled and crushed

150 g/5 oz carrots, scrubbed and diced

5 ml/1 tsp ground cinnamon

1 bay leaf

15 ml/1 tbsp fresh oregano leaves

500 g/18 oz tomatoes, skinned and roughly chopped

5 ml/1 tsp lemon juice

2 x 400 g/14 oz/large cans of butter (lima) beans, drained and rinsed

50 ml/2 fl oz/scant ¼ cup water

Sea salt and freshly ground black pepper

150 g/5 oz Feta cheese

30 ml/2 tbsp chopped fresh parsley

Heat the oil in a large frying pan. Add the onions, garlic and carrots and cook over a low heat, stirring occasionally, for about 20 minutes until soft and golden.

Preheat the oven to 180°C/350°F/gas 4 /fan oven 160°C.

Stir the cinnamon, herbs, tomatoes, lemon juice, beans, water and some seasoning into the onion mixture. Transfer it all to an ovenproof dish, cover with a lid or foil and bake for at least 1½–2 hours until the sauce is well reduced and coats the beans; stir it very gently every now and then, being careful not to mash the beans.

When it is all nice and thick, crumble the cheese over the top, sprinkle with the parsley and serve.

 This dish is also incredibly good served cold.

When we visited Tunisia several years ago, we were delighted with the wide range of vegetable dishes available on restaurant menus – beautifully fresh and sparkling salads, deeply savoury stews and bakes.

Chekchouka was a great favourite and, according to *La Sofra*, a lovely little cookery book I picked up in the Sousse market, each town and city has its very own version. Sometimes it turned up with poached or hard-boiled (hard-cooked) eggs sitting on top as a garnish, sometimes the eggs had been scrambled through the vegetables; on several occasions spicy Merguez sausage had been added. We thought the best chekchouka was the one topped with a baked egg, so that's what I've done here.

tunisian chekchouka

45 ml/3 tbsp olive oil

200 g/7 oz onions, peeled and thinly sliced

2 garlic cloves, peeled and crushed

1 small red (bell) pepper, about 150 g/5 oz, seeded and cut into 1 cm/$\frac{1}{2}$ in wide strips

1 small green pepper, about 150 g/5 oz, seeded and cut into 1 cm/$\frac{1}{2}$ in wide strips

1 small yellow pepper, about 150 g/5 oz, seeded and cut into 1 cm/$\frac{1}{2}$ in wide strips

5 ml/1 tsp cumin seeds, coarsely ground

5 ml/1 tsp sweet paprika

350 g/12 oz tomatoes, skinned and roughly chopped

Sea salt and freshly ground black pepper

2 eggs

30 ml/2 tbsp chopped fresh coriander (cilantro)

TO SERVE:

Pitta bread

Heat 30 ml/2 tbsp of the oil in a frying pan. Add the onions, garlic and peppers, cover with a lid and cook over a low heat for about 30 minutes until the vegetables are soft and starting to brown.

Stir in the cumin and paprika and cook for a couple of minutes, then add the tomatoes and some seasoning. Cover again and stew for a further 30 minutes.

Preheat the oven to 200°C/400°F/gas 6/fan oven 180°C. Transfer the contents of the frying pan to a baking dish and make two hollows with the back of a spoon.

Break the eggs carefully into the hollows and cook in the oven, uncovered, for 7–10 minutes, depending on how soft you like your yolks. Sprinkle the eggs with salt and pepper and drizzle them with the remaining oil. Strew the coriander over everything and serve immediately with some pitta bread to mop up the juices.

A very simple dish perhaps but oh, the flavours! Bold, robust, gutsy, full-bodied, vigorous, palate-tingling. Its southern European origins are unmistakable and, although its heartiness ensures its place in a winter kitchen, it is also terribly good for a summer barbecue, complementing grilled meat and fish to perfection.

And should you by any chance have any left over, it is delicious cold and is easy to pack and transport for a picnic.

penne with roasted vegetables and tomato tapenade

350 g/12 oz red onions, peeled and coarsely sliced

1 large red (bell) pepper, about 200 g/7 oz, seeded and cut into wide strips

1 large yellow pepper, about 200 g/7 oz, seeded and cut into wide strips

1 large aubergine (eggplant), about 350 g/12 oz, cut into chunks

250 g/9 oz courgettes (zucchini), cut into 1 cm/$\frac{1}{2}$ in discs

Whole unpeeled garlic cloves – as many as you want but at least 10!

Sea salt and freshly ground black pepper

60 ml/4 tbsp olive oil

250 g/9 oz wholemeal penne or other thick pasta

200 g/7 oz/1$\frac{3}{4}$ cups Feta cheese, crumbled

1 quantity of Roasted Fresh Tomato Tapenade (see page 118)

Preheat the oven to 200°C/400°F/gas 6/fan oven 180°C. Place all the vegetables in one or two large roasting tins, season them well and drizzle with the oil. Roast for about 1 hour, stirring occasionally, until they are soft and starting to blacken along the edges.

Cook the pasta in a large saucepan of salted boiling water according to the manufacturers' instructions and drain well. Return to the saucepan, gently fold in the roasted vegetables and sprinkle with the cheese.

Divide between two deep, warm plates, place a spoonful of tapenade on top and add more tapenade as you eat.

rotolo di caponata siciliama

Caponata is one of the glories of Sicilian vegetable cookery – silky aubergine stewed in olive oil, a hint of North Africa from the dried fruit and nuts, the bite of tart olives and capers – a hauntingly fragrant, sweet and sour combination. It is served as an antipasto but we also came across it in Sicily as a pasta sauce, and as a filling for calzone – which is where the idea for this rotolo was born.

The garlicky alioli is a very un-Sicilian accompaniment but it works exceptionally well, as does the Provençal Roasted Red Pepper Aioli on page 64, if you fancy that more.

20 g/³/₄ oz/3 tbsp pine nuts

60 ml/4 tbsp olive oil

250 g/9 oz aubergine (eggplant), cut into 1 cm/¹/₂ in chunks

150 g/5 oz onions, peeled and coarsely chopped

1 garlic clove, peeled and crushed

90 g/3¹/₂ oz celery (about 2 sticks), diced

Sea salt and freshly ground black pepper

350 g/12 oz tomatoes, skinned and coarsely chopped

50 g/2 oz dried apricots, diced

20 g/³/₄ oz raisins or sultanas (golden raisins)

5 ml/1 tsp runny honey

10 green olives, stoned (pitted) and quartered

30 ml/2 tbsp capers, rinsed and squeezed dry

4 sheets of filo pastry (paste), about 50 x 25 cm/20 x 10 in

30 g/1¹/₄ oz butter, melted

30 g/1¹/₄ oz freshly grated Parmesan cheese

1 quantity of Catalán Alioli (see page 146)

Preheat the oven to 160°C/325°F/gas 3/fan oven 145°C. Place the pine nuts on a baking (cookie) sheet and cook for 20 minutes until golden.

Heat half the oil in a large frying pan, add the aubergine and cook over a medium heat, stirring often, until it is browned and crusted.

Add the remaining olive oil, the onion, garlic and celery and continue to cook for a further 10 minutes.

Stir in some seasoning, the tomatoes, apricots, raisins or sultanas and honey. Lower the heat and cook gently, stirring occasionally, for 25–30 minutes until the tomatoes have totally broken down and the mixture is thick and quite dry.

Add the olives and capers and check the seasoning. Set aside for at least 30 minutes to cool.

Lay out a sheet of filo pastry on the worktop, keeping the others covered with a cloth as filo pastry dries out easily. Brush it with melted butter, then lay a second sheet on top of the first and brush again with butter. Repeat until you have four layers.

Stir the pine nuts into the caponata and spoon it in an even row along the length of the pastry rectangle, about 2 cm/³⁄₄ in from the edge closest to you and leaving a 3 cm/1¹⁄₄ in edge at each end. Fold the pastry up and over the caponata, enclosing it snugly, then carefully roll it all up into a tight sausage. Fold in the ends and place the rotolo on a baking (cookie) sheet, seam-side down. Sprinkle the Parmesan over the top.

Preheat the oven to 200°C/400°F/gas 6/fan oven 180°C and bake the rotolo for 30 minutes until it is crisp and golden. Slide it on to a warm serving dish and serve with the alioli. It doesn't slice particularly well so the easiest – if not the most elegant – way to deal with it is simply to cut it in half.

 The rotolo can be assembled the day before up to sprinkling with the Parmesan and chilled; bring it back to room temperature before cooking.

Try to find really richly coloured rhubarb so that you end up with an almost ridiculously bright pink fool. Rhubarb seems to have a surprising affinity to chocolate, in spite of its natural mouth-puckering acidity, so I always serve it with Dark Chocolate Chunk Cookies (opposite). They make a wonderful accompaniment!

bright pink
rhubarb fool

400 g/14 oz rhubarb

100 g/4 oz/$^{1}/_{2}$ cup caster (superfine) sugar

250 ml/8 fl oz/1 cup double (heavy) cream

Preheat the oven to 180°C/375°F/gas 5/fan oven 160°C.

Wash and dry the rhubarb, cut it into 2 cm/$^{3}/_{4}$ in lengths and place in a china baking dish. Sprinkle with the sugar and cook in the oven, uncovered, for about 30 minutes until it is soft – it will stew nicely in its own juices. Allow to cool slightly, then purée in a food processor or blender until fairly smooth. Set aside until completely cold.

Whip the cream until it forms soft peaks and gently fold in all but about 45 ml/3 tbsp of the rhubarb. Spoon the fool into two 250 ml/8 fl oz/1 cup ramekins (custard cups), drizzle the remaining purée over the top and chill until ready to serve.

This recipe makes about 16 cookies, so you will definitely have some over even though they are incredibly moreish. They are just as good the following day, by which time they will have lost their lovely crispness and acquired an equally alluring chewiness.

These cookies are delicious with my Bright Pink Rhubarb Fool (opposite).

dark chocolate chunk cookies

125 g/4¹/₂ oz/generous ¹/₂ cup unsalted (sweet) butter, at room temperature

90 g/3¹/₂ oz/scant ¹/₂ cup light brown sugar

90 g/3¹/₂ oz/scant ¹/₂ cup caster (superfine) sugar

1 large egg

2.5 ml/¹/₂ tsp vanilla essence (extract)

150 g/5 oz/1¹/₄ cups plain (all-purpose) flour

2.5 ml/¹/₂ tsp baking powder

2.5 ml/¹/₂ tsp sea salt

125 g/4¹/₂ oz dark chocolate (52% cocoa solids), coarsely chopped

Place the butter and two sugars in the bowl of a food processor and process until smooth and creamy. Add the egg and vanilla and process again.

Mix together the flour, baking powder and salt and add to the mixture in the food processor. Process briefly, just until mixed.

Scrape it all out into a large bowl and stir in the chocolate with a wooden spoon. Chill until firm – this will make it easier to shape before baking.

Preheat the oven to 190°C/375°F/gas 5/fan oven 170°C. Line one or two large baking (cookie) sheets with baking parchment. Take walnut-sized pieces of cookie dough, roll them into a ball between the palms of your hands and place them on the baking sheet about 3 cm/1¹/₄ in apart.

Bake in the oven for 8–10 minutes until they are light gold and the whole kitchen is rich with the aroma of chocolate and caramelising sugar. Allow the cookies to cool for 5 minutes before carefully transferring them with a large spatula to a wire rack to get completely cold.

 If you are not going to eat the cookies within a couple of hours, store them in an airtight container.

This recipe fills four ramekins –
two each as they are very moreish
– and, believe me, you *will* find
room for the second one. It would
obviously make more sense to put
them in two larger ramekins, but
they are not solid enough to set in
large quantities, and if you add
more cornflour they will lose their
lovely texture – so resist the
temptation!

summer berry cream pots under a chocolate crust

250 g/9 oz mixed berries – thawed frozen are fine

45 ml/3 tbsp Crème de Cassis

250 ml/8 fl oz/1 cup extra-thick cream

4 egg yolks

65 g/2$\frac{1}{2}$ oz caster (superfine) sugar

10 ml/2 tsp cornflour (cornstarch)

50 g/2 oz dark chocolate

FOR THE OPTIONAL GARNISH:

50 g/2 oz dark chocolate

6–8 long-stemmed strawberries

Place the berries in the bowl of a food processor with the Crème de Cassis and process until you have a smooth purée. Push the purée through a stainless steel or plastic sieve (strainer) to remove any seeds or pips.

Heat the cream in a small saucepan to just below boiling point.

Using an electric whisk, beat the egg yolks with the sugar and cornflour in a bowl on high speed until thick and pale. Turn down the speed to low and slowly pour on the hot cream, continuing to whisk until well blended. Return the mixture to the saucepan and cook, stirring constantly, until the mixture just boils. Remove from the heat and beat well with a wooden spoon until totally smooth.

Stir in the berry purée, place in a jug and pour carefully into four 120 ml/4 fl oz/ $\frac{1}{2}$ cup ramekins (custard cups). Allow to cool, then chill until totally cold and firm.

Melt the chocolate in a small bowl over boiling water until runny and then drizzle it with a teaspoon over the surface of the creams – do not make the chocolate crust too thick or you will have difficulty breaking through it once it has hardened.

To make the garnish, melt the chocolate in a small bowl over boiling water until runny. Holding the strawberries by their stems, dip them into the chocolate, twirl them around to coat them and let any excess drip off the end. Place them on a piece of greaseproof (waxed) paper or a plate lined with clingfilm (plastic wrap) to set.

Crema Catalana, the Catalán version of crème brûlée, is delicately flavoured with citrus zest and cinnamon, and, according to the waitress at Vinissim in the Barri Gotic of Barcelona (highly recommended!), not necessarily covered in a caramel crust. But the restaurant's frozen version definitely included crunchy caramel.

The chocolate chips are my addition – chop the chocolate quite finely so that it melts quickly on the tongue, adding yet another layer of flavour and texture.

I usually put ice cream for two straight from my ice-cream machine into ramekins as small quantities are fiddly to scoop.

crema catalana ice cream with caramel

250 ml/8 fl oz/1 cup double (heavy) cream

2 strips of lemon peel

2 strips of orange peel

1.5 ml/¼ tsp ground cinnamon

2 egg yolks

100 g/4 oz/½ cup caster (superfine) sugar

Oil for greasing

40 g/1¾ oz dark chocolate (52% cocoa solids), finely chopped

Place the cream in a small heavy-based saucepan with the orange and lemon peel and the cinnamon and heat gently until it is steaming.

In the meantime, whisk the egg yolks with half the sugar in a small bowl until thick and pale. Slowly pour on the hot cream, whisking all the time. Return the mixture to the saucepan and cook gently until it thickens, stirring constantly with a wooden spatula – do not let it boil or it will curdle. Remove from the heat and scrape it all into a clean bowl. Allow it to cool completely, then chill until totally cold – overnight is fine.

Grease a baking (cookie) sheet. Place the remaining sugar in a small heavy-based saucepan and add 45 ml/3 tbsp of water. Stir it over a low heat until the sugar has melted. Turn up the heat to medium and boil without stirring until the syrup is golden – watch it like a hawk as a small quantity of caramel like this will burn almost before you have realised it. Immediately pour the caramel on to the oiled sheet and leave it to cool and harden.

Remove the caramel from the tray and place in a freezer bag. Bash it gently with a rolling pin to break it up into very small pieces – if they are too big, they will be difficult to chew and you will break your teeth on them!

When the crema is nice and cold, discard the peel and churn it in an ice-cream machine according to the manufacturer's instructions, adding the caramel and chocolate a few minutes before it is ready. Divide it between two 120 ml/ 4 fl oz/½ cup ramekins (custard cups) and freeze until ready to serve.

Any summer berries can be used for this pavlova, but a mixture of raspberries and blueberries looks sensational. A decadently rich pudding, I admit, but utterly divine!

If you want to serve it in winter, try using bananas and mangoes instead of berries; they both go well with chocolate and, although the colours and presentation won't be quite so eye-catching, it will be just as delicious; and for the sauce, purée a very ripe mango and sharpen it with fresh lime juice and a dash of rum.

summer berry and chocolate pavlova

1 egg white

A pinch of salt

A pinch of cream of tartar

65 g/2^1/$_2$ oz icing (confectioners') sugar

5 ml/1 tsp cornflour (cornstarch)

2.5 ml/^{1}/$_2$ tsp cider vinegar or white wine vinegar

100 g/4 oz dark chocolate (52% cocoa solids)

200 ml/7 fl oz/scant 1 cup double (heavy) cream

200 g/7 oz summer berries

FOR THE SAUCE:

200 g/7 oz raspberries (thawed frozen is fine)

50 g/2 oz/^{1}/$_4$ cup caster (superfine) sugar

60 ml/4 tbsp Crème de Cassis

TO SERVE:

Double cream

Preheat the oven to 140°C/275°F/gas 1/fan oven 125°C. Line a baking (cookie) sheet with baking parchment and draw two circles about 13 cm/5 in diameter on it.

Place the egg white in a small bowl, add the salt and cream of tartar and whisk with an electric beater until stiff. Whisk in the icing sugar, a little at a time, until the mixture is thick and glossy. Whisk in the cornflour (cornstarch) and the vinegar.

Using a spatula, spread the meringue on the circles on the baking parchment. Bake for 30 minutes until they turn pale gold. Set aside to cool.

To make the sauce, place all the ingredients in a food processor and process until smooth. Push the purée through a nylon or stainless steel sieve (strainer) to remove the pips.

Put the chocolate in a small glass or china bowl and melt it over a pan of hot water. Allow to cool to barely warm but still runny. Whisk the cream until stiff and gently fold in the cooled chocolate.

Spread the chocolate cream over each meringue, arrange the berries on top and serve with the sauce and extra cream.

 The baked meringue rounds will keep well in an airtight container for several days. The sauce can be prepared 2 or 3 days in advance and chilled.

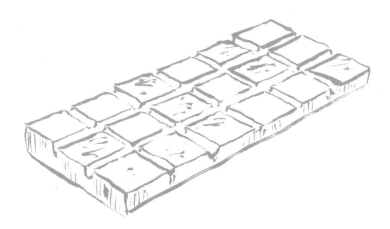

twice-baked muscat raisin and chocolate soufflés

You will need two china ramekins (custard cups) and individual gratin dishes for this recipe.

Chopping the chocolate quite coarsely results in small pools of soft chocolate melting through the soufflé, and its faint bitterness enhances the distinctive flavour of the Muscat wine.

You do not need an expensive dessert wine for this – Moscatel de Valencia will do. But some of the better ones come in half bottles and there will be just enough left over to drink with the soufflés.

Once you have tried this soufflé, you may want to have a go at one of the delicious savoury options on pages 126–9.

60 g/2½ oz raisins

250 ml/8 fl oz/1 cup sweet Muscat wine

20 g/¾ oz unsalted (sweet) butter

20 g/¾ oz/3 tbsp plain (all-purpose) flour

120 ml/4 fl oz/½ cup milk

2 eggs, separated

30 g/1¼ oz dark chocolate (minimum 52% cocoa solids), coarsely chopped

A pinch of cream of tartar

30 g/1¼ oz caster (superfine) sugar

Butter for greasing

250 ml/8 fl oz/1 cup double (heavy) cream

Place the raisins and wine in a small saucepan, bring to the boil and simmer gently until the raisins have absorbed most of the liquid. Allow to cool slightly, then purée coarsely in a food processor.

Melt the butter in a small saucepan over a medium heat and stir in the flour. Cook, stirring, for a few minutes until the mixture looks like wet sand.

Slowly whisk in the milk and bring it to the boil, stirring all the time, then simmer for a couple of minutes. Allow to cool to lukewarm, then stir in the egg yolks, raisin purée and chocolate. Set aside to cool completely.

Preheat the oven to 200°C/400°F/gas 6/fan oven 180°C. Whisk the egg whites with the cream of tartar until it forms firm peaks, then whisk in the sugar. Carefully fold into the soufflé base.

Grease two 250 ml/8 fl oz/1 cup china ramekins (custard cups) and line the bases with a round of baking parchment. Divide the mixture between the ramekins and place them in a roasting tin half-filled with hot water. Bake for 30 minutes until well risen and golden.

Remove from the water bath and allow cool completely. (The soufflés can be prepared up to this point and chilled for 24 hours; bring them back to room temperature before the second bake.)

Preheat the oven to 200°C/400°F/gas 6/fan oven 180°C. Unmould the soufflés by carefully running a small knife around the inside and turning them out on to the palm of your hand – be very gentle as they are delicate. Remove the baking parchment and place them, browned-sides up, in two gratin dishes about 13 cm/5 in across. (A single one large enough to hold them both with 3 cm/1¼ in between each will work, though they will be a little more difficult to serve.)

Pour half the cream over them and bake for 25 minutes until they are all puffed up again and the cream is bubbling and starting to brown.

Serve immediately with the remaining cream.

Chaussons aux Pommes are one of the first things I look for when I am in Normandy. They are made with wonderfully light, buttery puff pastry and the best pâtisseries always put a big dollop of thick Normandy cream in with the apple filling. If you manage to time your purchase accurately and the chausson is still warm from the oven, it is quite heavenly.

I seldom get around to making my own puff pastry and commercial puff pastry never has the right texture or flavour, so I use filo for my version of chausson. I also add chocolate chips to the filling – more American than Norman but incredibly good.

apple turnovers with caramel sauce

FOR THE CARAMEL SAUCE:

125 g/4$\frac{1}{2}$ oz/generous $\frac{1}{2}$ cup caster (superfine) sugar

100 ml/3$\frac{1}{2}$ fl oz/scant $\frac{1}{2}$ cup water

120 ml/4 fl oz/$\frac{1}{2}$ cup double (heavy) cream

FOR THE TURNOVERS:

1 small eating (dessert) apple, about 100 g/4 oz

40 g/1$\frac{3}{4}$ oz dark chocolate (52% cocoa solids)

20 g/$\frac{3}{4}$ oz/3 tbsp chopped, toasted hazelnuts (filberts)

15 ml/1 tbsp caster sugar

2 sheets of filo pastry (paste), about 40 x 28 cm/16 x 11 in

20 g/$\frac{3}{4}$ oz unsalted (sweet) butter, melted

5 ml/1 tsp icing (confectioners') sugar (optional)

TO SERVE:

Thick cream (optional)

To make the sauce, place the sugar and water in a small saucepan and bring to the boil, stirring constantly to dissolve the sugar. Let it boil on medium heat, without stirring, until golden – watch it carefully at this stage as it will burn in the blink of an eye.

Remove it from the heat and carefully add the cream, standing well back because it will hiss and splutter (I find it helps to wear rubber gloves for this part of the exercise!). Whisk until smooth and set aside to cool.

To make the turnovers, peel, core and dice the apple into pieces no larger than 1 cm/$\frac{1}{2}$ in. Do the same with the chocolate, and place them both in a small bowl. Stir in the hazelnuts and sugar.

Lay one sheet of filo pastry on a work surface and, using a pastry brush, brush with melted butter. Cover with the second filo sheet and brush again with butter. Cut the double sheet in half lengthways into two strips.

Place half the apple mixture about 5 cm/2 in from the end of each strip. Fold the 5 cm/2 in flap up and over the apples, bringing the left-hand corner across to the right to form a triangle. Fold the triangle up and then over to the left, and continue up the strip, turning each triangle across and over. Place the two pastry parcels on a baking (cookie) sheet lined with foil or baking parchment.

Preheat the oven to 180°C/350°F/gas 4/fan oven 160°C and cook for 30 minutes until crisp and brown. Dust with the icing sugar, if you like, and serve with the caramel sauce – and extra cream if you are feeling greedy!

The contrast of textures in a hot charlotte is pure alchemy: smooth filling, crisp, crunchy bread case, velvety custard, thick unctuous cream…

The golden rule when making a charlotte, whether sweet or savoury, is to make sure the filling is thick and quite dry, so cook it right down until it is stiff enough to stand a spoon in. If the filling is at all sloppy, it will leak out into the bread and soften it, and your charlotte will quite simply disintegrate when you turn it out.

apricot charlottes with apricot custard

200 ml/7 fl oz/scant 1 cup milk

2 egg yolks

90 g/3½ oz/scant ½ cup caster (superfine) sugar

45 ml/3 tbsp apricot brandy or liqueur

500 g/18 oz fresh apricots, halved and stoned (pitted)

65 g/2½ oz unsalted (sweet) butter, melted

30 ml/2 tbsp demerara sugar

About 6 large slices of thinly sliced wholemeal bread

Extra-thick cream (optional)

Heat the milk in a small saucepan until steaming and frilly around the edges. Beat the egg yolks and 15 ml/1 tbsp of the caster sugar in a small bowl with an electric beater until pale and thick. Slowly beat in the hot milk. Pour it all back into the saucepan and cook over a medium heat, stirring constantly with a wooden spatula, until the custard thickens and coats the back of the spatula. Pour it into a clean bowl, stir in 15 ml/1 tbsp of the apricot brandy or liqueur and set aside to cool.

Put the apricots and the remaining caster sugar in a heavy-based saucepan. Add 30 ml/2 tbsp of water and the remaining apricot brandy or liqueur and bring to the boil. Turn the heat right down, cover the saucepan and let the apricots cook for 10 minutes, by which time they should have broken down into a mush.

Turn up the heat to medium and let them cook, uncovered, stirring often, until they have reduced to a thick purée. This will take about 30 minutes. Make sure there is no liquid left or the charlottes will collapse when you unmould them.

Meanwhile, grease two 250 ml/8 fl oz/1 cup metal ramekins (custard cups) with a little of the melted butter and line the bases with a round of baking parchment. Sprinkle the demerara sugar into the ramekins and twirl them around to coat the sides with the sugar.

Cut out two bread circles to fit the bottoms of the ramekins, brush both sides with melted butter, and press them firmly into the ramekins. Cut some more bread into wide strips, again brush both sides with melted butter, and use them lengthways to line the sides of the ramekins, overlapping them as necessary to create a 'case' with no gaps between the slices. Now cut out two more bread circles to fit snugly into the top of the ramekins, inside the bread cases.

When the apricot purée is ready, whisk 30 ml/2 tbsp into the custard and spoon the rest into the bread cases – if you have any left over, add it to the custard. Push the bread lids firmly in place on top of the purée.

Preheat the oven to 200°C/400°F/gas 6/fan oven 180°C. Stand the ramekins on a baking (cookie) sheet and bake the charlottes for 30 minutes. Remove them from the oven and let them rest for 10 minutes before unmoulding them carefully on to two warm plates.

Serve with the apricot custard and some cold, thick cream if you wish.

This is the kind of pudding one loses oneself in. Whenever I eat it, I find myself dreamily drifting along on its textures: the smoothness, the crunchiness, the richness, the utter sensuousness! Definitely a pudding for times when you crave a bit of self-indulgence.

Caramel can be treacherous, so give it your full attention while it is cooking – and it is a good idea to wear rubber gloves as the smallest fleck of boiling caramel on bare skin can be very painful indeed.

rich and sensuous toffee dream

50 g/2 oz/¼ cup caster (superfine) sugar, plus extra for sprinkling

75 ml/5 tbsp water

200 ml/7 fl oz/scant 1 cup double (heavy) cream

2 egg yolks

5 ml/1 tsp cornflour (cornstarch)

Place the sugar and water in a small heavy-based saucepan. Bring it to the boil, stirring all the time to dissolve the sugar. As soon as it boils, turn the heat down to medium and let it cook until it turns a warm gold colour – stand over it as this will happen very quickly and it will go from warm gold to burned in a trice.

Remove the saucepan from the heat, stand well back and pour in the cream, which will hiss and splutter like mad. When the excitement has subsided, stir the mixture well to dissolve the caramelised sugar completely. Set aside.

Place the egg yolks and cornflour in a small bowl and whisk with an electric beater until thick. Carefully pour on the toffee cream, whisking all the time. Pour it all back into the saucepan and cook it on a low heat, stirring constantly, until it just boils and thickens. If any lumps have formed, whisk it again with the electric beater.

Strain the mixture into a jug and pour it carefully into two 120 ml/4 fl oz/½ cup china ramekins (custard cups). Allow to cool, then chill until totally cold.

About 15 minutes before you plan to eat the dreams, sprinkle 15 ml/1 tbsp of sugar over each one and caramelise the tops either with a blow torch or under a hot grill (broiler). Return them to the fridge for 10 minutes to firm them up again before serving.

index